Evil Defined

From A Christian Perspective

Roger J. Boehm, DCC, Ph.D.

Roger J. Boehm, Ph.D.

Titusville, FL

cfcc@lwol.com

Copyright 2006 by Roger J. Boehm

ISBN 978-0-6151-3489-5

Contents

About the Author

D r. Roger Boehm holds six earned degrees, all Summa Cum Laude, which include a Graduate of Biblical Studies and a Bachelor of Ministry in Christian Counseling from Bethany Bible College; a Master of Ministry in Christian Counseling, Doctor of Christian Counseling, and Ph.D. in Religion with a Christian Counseling Concentration from Bethany Theological Seminary; and a Ph.D. in Clinical Christian Psychology from Cornerstone University.

He is the Executive Director of the Center for Christian Counseling and Training in Titusville, Florida.

He has served as a chaplain in a 1200 prisoner facility, conducted mission work, evangelistic meetings, and pastoral training in the countries of Haiti and Cameroon, West Africa; pastored churches in 5 states; and conducted seminars, evangelistic meetings and revivals in 14 states from California to Florida.

As a Christian Counselor Dr. Boehm is licensed through the National Christian Counselors Association as a Clinical Pastoral Counselor Advanced Certification. He is a Diplomate and Board certified as a Clinical Supervisor and Board certified in the areas of Sexual Therapy, Marriage and Family Therapy, and Child & Adolescent Therapy with the National Board of Christian Clinical Therapists.

Dr. Boehm has authored a number of other books and pamphlets including the book *In the Face of Evil – A Wakeup Call for Christians*.

He and his wife Diane currently reside in Titusville, Florida.

I gratefully dedicate this reference book to my Lord Jesus Christ, my Savior and Redeemer – my friend, and my Wonderful Counselor.

I also dedicate this reference book to my wife, Diane, who I love very much. She is my wonderful partner, lover and my best earthly friend. Without her support and encouragement this book would have been impossible to write.

I give a special acknowledgment to Amy Holmes who spent countless hours typing and retyping. Her work on this reference book proved to be invaluable.

And to Rev. C.L. Powers and other men of God who taught me the Holy Scriptures and encouraged me along the way.

Thank you all so very much.

In Ephesians 6:10-17 we are taught that
in the believer's experience of union with the Lord Jesus
will be fought
the keenest and closest battles
with Satan and his hosts.

Finally, be strong in the Lord and in his mighty power.
Put on the full armor of God so that you can
take your stand against the devil's schemes.
For our struggle is not against flesh and blood,
but against the rulers,
against the authorities,
against the powers of this dark world
and against the spiritual forces of evil in the
heavenly realms.
Therefore put on the full armor of God,
so that when the day of evil comes,
you may be able to stand your ground,
and after you have done everything,
to stand.
Stand firm then,
with the belt of truth buckled around your waist,
with the breastplate of righteousness in place,
and with your feet fitted with the readiness that comes
from the gospel of peace.
In addition to all this, take up the shield of faith,
with which you can extinguish all the flaming arrows
of the evil one.
Take the helmet of salvation and the sword of the Spirit,
which is the word of God.

x

Introduction

We live in a world full of evil deceptions wrapped in fine linen, so that if we aren't careful we will be deceived. Satan is the great deceiver and his job is to kill, steal, and destroy

Our youth are involved in such activities as Harry Potter, Magic cards, and lucid dreaming. Some are even joining Satanic and Wicca groups and involved in such activities as casting spells as well as human and animal sacrifices. Often parents see symbols or hear certain words with no understanding of their meaning while their youth dabble in darkness right before their eyes.

Adults, even Christians, join organizations and get involved in such activities as Yoga and Acupuncture with no idea they are dabbling in darkness. Others are involved in organizations they are deceived into believing are Christian, when in reality these organizations are evil by nature.

This reference book is meant to be a guide to the dark side from a Christian perspective for pastors, church leaders, parents, and others.

It is my prayer that through referencing this book Christians will avoid dabbling in the occult. Hopefully they will be better able to understand the evil around us, and will use this book as a reference in communicating to others the evil pitfalls of activities they may find themselves considering, or even already involved in, so that they might avoid the spiritual dangers by ceasing evil activities.

Reader Please Note!

Many of these definitions deal with the occult. You may notice their meanings to be completely different in other contexts. Remember, Satan counterfeits the things of God.

A

ACUPUNCTURE: Acupuncture is an occult practice. It is an ancient Chinese treatment dating back several thousand years. The term means, "to puncture with a needle" *(acus:* needle, and *punctura:* puncture*)*. The treatment involves the inserting of fine needles into the body at various points, which are revolved or left in place for a certain period of time. Needles normally range from one to ten inches in length and are made of gold, silver, platinum, or of steel. Acupuncture is used to relieve pain, to anaesthetize a patient during surgery, and to treat conditions ranging from arthritis to digestive problems.

The question is whether or not acupuncture should be classified as occult because of its pagan religious and philosophical associations. The treatment is based upon the pagan cosmic principle of *Yin* and *Yang* from ancient China. In the Oriental pseudoscience of acupuncture there is the idea of the need of maintaining the balance of vital energy and vital source of Yin and Yang in the body. Yin and Yang, according to Chinese philosophy, constitute the male and female cosmic forces in the universe from which everything derives its existence. This ancient Oriental philosophy teaches that this cosmic duality is also expressed as good and evil, pleasure and pain, hot and cold, and so on. In the healing system of acupuncture the key to life and health is the maintenance of harmony between Yin and the Yang within the body. By inserting needles along the network of meridians that connect the 12 vital organs, the acupuncturist seeks to bring the flow of vital energy back to its normal balance.

The Chinese explain it all in terms of the Yin and the Yang principle from their ancient pagan philosophy. As one author observes, acupuncture, which began as a folk method of healing, developed its own *occult mystique,* some of which is still connected with the healing process. In addition to the Yin and Yang philosophy there is found in the practice of acupuncture a stress upon the mystique of key numbers (e.g., 5 and 12), mystical ideas and concepts (such as "cosmic harmony," the "Gate of Life," the *chi* force), and the use of pulse diagnosis. Acupuncturists who are adept at pulse diagnosis frequently are able not only to diagnose present ailments (by reading 12 pulses serving 12 organs, not simply the wrist pulse), but can also look into the past and discover previous ailments. All this has caused some occultists to surmise that acupuncture seems to have a *psychic dimension* somewhat in common with that of clairvoyants and mediums with ESP powers. Some suggest the acupuncturist has a psychic gift enabling him to discern vibrations from the pulse that would go unrecognized by others. *Acupuncture definitely has occult associations.*

AKASHIC RECORDS: In occultism said to be cosmic records in the form of scenic representations of every thought, word, or action which has taken place since the world began. These records are believed to contain the complete activities of every being, as well as every event in minute detail both past and present. This theory is often advanced as the method by which psychics and clairvoyants receive the hidden information about a person or event. Some, as Edgar Cayce and Arthur Ford, were said to have had access to these "records" to a remarkable degree. They are supposed to have availed themselves of the information in these records while in a state of trance. The advocates of the unscriptural doctrine of reincarnation also contend that consultations of these records can be made in order to discover one's alleged "past lives," and the present "debt of Karma" he is working out in his present life.

Actually, such information is derived from demonic sources. Deceiving spirits generally have considerable knowledge of the past and present, or have supernatural means of obtaining it, and they seduce the gullible by supplying them with information (both true and false) from these supposed "Akashic Records."

ALMANAC: The term *almanac* (or almanack) is derived from the Arabic, meaning "timetable or calendar of the heavens." Almanacs in one form or another date from ancient times and have occult associations. The occult nature of almanacs in general is found in their reliance upon astrology, the influence of the zodiac upon human life and agriculture, moon phase weather forecasting, the lunar superstitions concerning planting and gardening, folklore, lucky numbers and days, fortunetelling, charms, and many other superstitions.

Some scientific and factual information can be found in the pages of most almanacs, such as tables of annual eclipses, tidal information, table of weight and measures, and cooking recipes. However, Christians should refrain from using almanacs because of their occult nature which could possibly have adverse influences upon those who read them.

ALPHABETS (OCCULT): Many forms of writing are utilized in the occult. You should be aware that spirit writing, writing backwards, symbolic writing and writings uniquely characteristic to a particular group may be used. Variations to any alphabet may also occur.

AMULET, CHARM, FETISH, GOOD-LUCK SYMBOL, TALISMAN: A supposed preservative against sickness, accident, witchcraft, and evil spirits or demons. Amulets consist of precious stones, gems, gold, and sometimes of parchment written over with some inscription. They have been widely used from remote antiquity. They are usually worn as earrings, or as a necklace. The English word "Amulet" does not occur in Scripture, but the word "charms"; Isaiah 3:20 (NIV) is generally understood to have the meaning of amulets. They also formed the part of the trappings which Jacob commanded his household to put away in Genesis 35:4 (rings in the ear).

APPORT MAGIC: The transference of objects through closed doors or sealed containers by means of the penetration of matter. Supernatural appearances and disappearances of material images in connection with the activities of a Spiritistic Medium.

ASTRAL OR SOUL TRAVEL: The practice of sending your soul on an out-of-body journey to distant places to discover hidden things. This is a common practice among more advanced New Age and Eastern religion practitioners and Spiritistic Mediums. But Christians have also been known to practice soul travel.

ASTROLOGY: An ancient art or pseudoscience which claims to forecast events on earth, human character, and man's fate by observation of the fixed stars and of the sun, moon, and planets.

AURA: An apparent envelope or field of colored radiation said to surround the human body and other animate objects, with the color or colors indicating different aspects of the person's physical, psychological, and spiritual conditions (see also Kirilian). The human aura, according to psychics, consists of a series of seven layers of radiation (emanations of light) surrounding the body. These emanations may be compared to the heat waves radiating from a stove, or the light rays surrounding a street lamp at night. The aura is said to reveal the physical, mental, emotional, and spiritual condition of an individual. Man, according to occult belief, consists of seven principles: physical body; astral body; vital force; instinctive mind; intellect; spiritual mind; and spirit. Each of these principles supposedly sends forth energy in the form of emanations of various colors of light (the aura), and is designated as the "health" aura, the "astral" aura, and so on.

AUSTROMANCY: Divination by studying the winds.

AUTOEROTIC ASPHYXIATION / AUTOEROTIC STIMULATION: The sinful practice of inducing cerebral anoxia, usually by means of self-applied ligatures or suffocating devices, while the individual masturbates to orgasm. Of the various types of abnormal sexual behavior probably the most bizarre and dangerous is autoerotic asphyxiation, also known as sexual hanging.

Some breath control advocates say that what they do is acceptably safe because they do not take what they do to the point of unconsciousness. But with asphyxiation it is hard to tell when a person is about to be unconscious until they actually become so. Therefore it's extremely difficult to know when the actual point of unconsciousness will occur until it is reached and the person is asphyxiated. So then why do people practice autoerotic asphyxiation? Because they report that when the asphyxiation starts to occur they get an enormous high. When an individual tries asphyxiation while they are having sex they seem to get an everlasting orgasm. It is thought that when the actions are slowed down by the asphyxiation the feeling seems to take longer.

Breath control cannot be done in a way that is not life threatening, but then Satan's job is to kill, steal, and destroy. The risk of experimenting with breath control play is enormous. At times the individual passes out and dies. Often to protect the family these instances are reported as suicide with no additional details given. Also known as scarfing and sexual hanging.

AUTOMATIC WRITING: Writing done while in a trance – ostensibly containing supernatural and prophetic messages. The pen is held in the hand but is directed by spiritual forces. The finished product is often in a hand-written style or language other than that of the one holding the pen.

AVERSE: Black of evil.

AVATAR: A Person who "descends" into human form from above as a manifestation of divinity and who reveals divine truth to people. Such a one has supposedly progressed beyond the need to be reincarnated in another body (i.e., there is no further "bad Karma" to work off).

An incarnation of the godhead in human flesh, according to Hindu teaching that occurs when mankind is spiritually confused and needs direction: Drishna, Buddha, Mohammed and Christ are all considered to be avatars.

AWARENESS: Thought to be an "exalted state of consciousness", usually achieved by meditation, in which one becomes aware of entities and spiritual energies.

AXIOMANCY: Divination by observation of the quivers of an ax or hatchet.

AYURVEDA: Five-thousand-year old Hindu life science, considered the mother of healing arts, using yoga, diet, Tantrism, and Vedantic philosophy.

B

BAAL: The chief god of the Canaanites.

BAAL-BERITH: "Lord of the Covenant"; A Canaanite god.

BAALIM: Masters or Arch demons- see Masters of Wisdom for names.

BAAL-PEOR: "Lord of the opening"; A Moabite god of uncleanness; also referred to as "Peor".

BAALZEBUB: A Hebrew name that means "Lord of the Flies"; in the Old Testament, the god of Ekron (see Beelzebub).

BAALZEPHON: In demonology, captain of the guard and sentinels of hell.

BACULUM: A witch's wand, staff or broom stick.

BAHIR: A source book of the Cabala; presents some of the basic teachings of Judaic mysticism.

BALEFIRE: Ritual coven fire.

BAPHOMET: At one time was worshipped by the Knights Templar and later by those who took part in the black mass. Today it is seen as a deity, a goat-headed god with angelic wings, the breasts of a female, and an illuminated torch between his horns.

BAR-JESUS: Full of all deceit and all fraud, son of the devil, enemy of all righteousness.

BARROW: An Elven or Celtic burial mound.

BASILISK: A legendary dragon, serpent, or lizard whose breath or look was considered fatal.

BEELZEBUB: Traditionally one of the most powerful evil spirits; ranking in importance with Lucifer, Ashtaroth, Satan. Thought of as an evil spirit of decay. Often thought to rank directly under Satan himself.

BEL: The chief Babylonian deity.

BELIAL: This evil spirit is considered to be the most vicious of all the evil spirits. He is identified with death and evil. He is a spirit of destruction.

BELL: Rung to begin and end rituals. Also used as a trigger for Satanic Ritual Abuse victims.

BELOMANAY-RABDOMANCY: Divination by tossing or balancing arrows.

BELTANE: Celtic, pre-Christian spring festival, celebrated on May Day. One of the major witches' Sabbaths. A fertility festival that is one of the witches' major holidays.

BHAGAVAD GITA: Sanskrit poem relating a dialogue between Lord Krishna and Arjuna consistent of 700 2-line stanzas in 18 chapter; part of Krishna's revelation called an Upanishad, which is a succinct summary of dominant themes in Hindu theology. Hindu sacred scripture.

BILIOMANCY: Divination by books.

BIND: To cast a spell on someone or something.

BIOFEEDBACK: Technique using instruments to self-monitor normally unconscious, involuntary body processes such as brain waves, heartbeat and muscle tension. As this information is fed back to the person, he or she can then consciously and voluntarily control internal biological functions.

BIORHYTHM: An occult explanation for the rhythmical recurrence of physical and psychological tendencies, presuming the existence of a precise regularity used to chart behavior.

BLACK BRADON: A popular grimoire attributed to Honrius, an occultist of the 15th century.

BLACK MAGIC: Used for blighting or binding. Popularly, magick done for "evil" purposes.

BLACK MASS: The most diabolical ritual that is performed by the Satanist. It is a communion with Satan, involving the desecration of all sacred objects used in the Christian Lord's Supper. It also can include the sacrifice of an unbaptized infant. A satanic religious ceremony which honors Satan and denigrates Jesus.

BLACK METAL MUSIC: Themes include: the death of God; sex with corpses; human sacrifices; sitting at Satan's left hand; calling Jesus the deceiver; and glorifying the name of Satan.

"BLACK POPE": A reference to Anton LaVey; former high priest of the Church of Satan.

BLACK PULLET: A grimoire that probably dates from the late 1700's.

BLACK WIDOW SPIDER: Mark of death.

"BLESSED BE": Phrase used by witches both as a greeting and as a farewell. Note: "So Moot it be" (used in Freemasonry) may be used as well.

BLIGHTING: The use of psychic energy to harm or destroy an organism.

BLOOD: Is the life force. The Satanist believes that by drinking another person's blood or the blood of an animal, it will transfer that life force to the Satanist magnifying the force several times.

BLOOD PACT - A pledge to Satan signed with blood from the person making the promise.

BLOOD SUBSCRIPTIONS: Using one's own blood to subscribe or to commit in a signed statement one's life to Satan. (Also to sign a contract with Satan.)

BLUE MAGIC: Used for emotional work, love, etc. Peace and protection.

BODHISATTVA: A being who has supposedly earned the right to enter into Nirvana or into illumination, but instead voluntarily turns back from that state in order to help humanity in attaining the same goal. Jesus Christ is thought to be a Bodhisattva.

BODYWORK: Rather than simple development of the outer musculature, this approach to fitness aims to reduce muscular tensions in search of "psychic freedom" by using complex yoga-like physical exercises and postures.

BOOK OF CHANGES: (See I Ching)

BOOK OF (THE) DEAD: An Egyptian handbook for guiding the souls of the dead through the underworld.

BOOK OF ENOCH: A work, apparently written in the 2nd century B.C., which forms the basis for much of the mythology with witchcraft.

BOOK OF MOSES: The standard magician's code of the Middle Ages; it contains a complicated ritual for induction of neophytes.

BOOK OF SHADOWS: In witchcraft, the personal book of spells, rituals, and folklore a witch compiles after being initiated into the coven. The Book of Shadows is kept secret and, traditionally, is destroyed when the witch dies.

BOOK OF TOTH/THOTH: A book containing the wisdom of the Egyptian gods; possibly the origin for the Tarot.

BOTANOMANCY: Divination by burning tree branches and leaves.

BOTANICA: Occult shop serving the magickal needs of the Afro-Catholic communities of Voudoun, Macumba, Santeria, etc. Botanicas sell herbs, spells, charms, votive candles, images of saints, etc.

BOUL: Ruler of the West.

BRAHMAN: In Hinduism, the principal and ultimate reality, which is identical with all that is.

BREEDER: A woman who bears a child to be used for ritual sacrifice. Impregnated by male members of the coven approximately 4 months prior to a required human sacrifice in accord with the Satanic Ritual Calendar (pp. 125-128), at the appointed date and ceremony the infant is aborted and immediately sacrificed to Satan as a human sacrifice. Since there was no recorded birth there is no record of anyone missing. Interestingly enough, Satan accepts an aborted fetus as a human being/sacrifice and has deceived many into believing it is just so much fetal tissue and not a human being at this stage and therefore abortion is acceptable.

BRIGID: A witch festival held on February 2nd Eve.

BRIGIT: Great Celtic Triple Goddess. She is matron of: the forge and smithcraft; poetry and inspiration; healing and medicine. Christianized as St. Brigit, her festival is Candlemas or Oimeic, Feb. 2nd.

BRUJERIA: A Mexican magical system that is an amalgamation of Catholicism and native Indian lore; a sort of synthetic mestizo-shamanism. A male practitioner is called a Brujo, a female is a Bruja. These people are apt to be urban dwellers who burn candles to both saints and demons with equal facility, they gain their magickal powers through self-initiation, sometimes with training. Though they often claim the more benign title of Curandro (a healer) their practices may run the gamut from love spells to curses.

BUDDHA: "The Enlightened One." An avatar or messenger.

C

CABALA (KABBALAH): Occult material that apparently originated in Chaldea and Mesopotamia and was incorporated into ancient Jewish works and traditions; also refers to practices of magic that are derived from those works.

CADUCEUS: The serpent-entwined herald's staff of Hermes/Mercury. As it was also the wizard's staff of the Greek physician Aesculapius, it has become the symbol of the medical profession.

CALF WORSHIP: Calves and bulls figured prominently in Egyptian mythology and the Israelites, in demanding a golden calf, may have been recalling Egyptian idols or perhaps were just adopting a well-known god-symbol. Every king after Jeroboam carried on sacrifices to the gold calves that Jeroboam made.

CANCER: An astrological sign (in the months of June and July).

CANDLEMAS: See Brigid.

CANDLES: Used in all rituals and ceremonies, the color reflecting the type ritual. Black is the color associated with the devil.

CANNIBAL: A person who eats the flesh of human beings.

CANTRIP: A spell cast by a witch. A written spell or charm that reads the same forwards or backwards.

CAPNOMANCY: Divination by observing smoke as it rises from a fire, such as from a burnt sacrifice or from incense.

CARD LAYING: A widespread means of fortune-telling; the obviously fraudulent and money making types, the suggestive and telepathic fortune-telling types, and the mediumistic types of card-laying based on extrasensory and demonic faculties.

CHARMING: Treatment by magic, a matter of sorcery.

CARTOMANCY: Divination or fortune-telling by means of cards.

CATHARI: From the term "cat" whose posterior they kiss and in whose form Satan appears to them.

CATS: Associated with the moon, night, wisdom, and healing. The Egyptian goddess of music, dance and celebration of life primarily in the Pagan/Neo-Pagan traditions.

CATOPTROMANCY: Divination by means of gazing at a mirror tilted towards the sun.

CAULDRON: A large pot used even today by practitioners. The opening in the cauldron represents the female womb. The cauldron is a very sacred object to practitioners.

CAUSIMOMANCY: Divination by observing how an object placed in fire burns or fails to burn.

CAYCE, EDGAR: The so-called sleeping prophet who, while resting, entered trance states in which he foretold future events, philosophized about such occult subjects as reincarnation, and purported to give cures for various ills.

CELEBRANT: The presiding priest at a ceremony.

CENTURIES: A French physician and occultist whose esoteric poetry many believe foretold events of modern history.

CEPHALOMANCY: Divination by using the head or skull of a donkey or goat.

CERANUOSCOPY: Observation of thunder and lightning for signs or omens.

CEROSCOPY: Melted wax is poured into cold water, and the resulting shapes are interpreted as a means of divination.

CEREBERUS: Three headed dog that guarded the entrance of hell.

CERNUNNOS: Latin "horned one." Ancient Celtic version of the Horned God, shown with stag antlers. Collective spirit of the wild animals. Equated with **FAUNUS**, the Red Man.

CHAKAM: A Hebrew word for "wise".

CHAKKIM: A Hebrew word for "wise one".

CHALDEAN ORACLES: Oracles and mystical sayings allegedly deriving from the Chaldean Magi and Zoroaster, but transcribed and translated by the Neoplatonist. Commentaries on the Oracles were written by Psellus, Pletho, Iamblicus, and Porphyry. The Oracles have much in common with Gnosticism.

CHALICE: Cup or goblet symbolized woman in ritual use; can contain sacrificial blood, wine or water. A goblet which can be made of glass or metal, but is always silver in color. Among Satanists, gold is the symbol of righteousness. A consecrated ceremonial cup, representing the Element Water, and containing the liquid sacrament of communion, usually wine.

CHAMMANIM: Images of the Sun.

CHANNELING: Process of receiving information from some level of reality other than the ordinary physical one and from beyond the "self" as it is generally understood. A "channeler", or medium, usually goes into a trance to establish contact with a spirit, ascended master, higher consciousness, or some other entity, and then receives and repeats messages from "the other side" of the physical world.

CHAKRAS: The seven energy points on the human body, according to new Agers and yogi(s). "Raising" the Kundalini up through the chakras is the aim of yoga meditation. Enlightenment (samandhi) is achieved when kundalini reaches the "crown chakra" at the top of the head.

CHANNELING (SPEAKING IN A TRANCE) - Under the control of demonic power a Spiritistic medium loses consciousness and deceptively imitates communication with the dead.

CHAPTERS: Branches of church organization.

CHARM: In magic, an incantation or object believed to have special supernatural power. The word derives from the Latin Carmen, meaning "a song". Compare with **TALISMAN**.

CHARTOM (CHARTUMMIN): A Hebrew term derived from Egyptian, meaning "men learned in sacred writings, rituals, spells".

CHEMOSH: A national idol of the Moabites and the Ammonites, has been identified with **BAAL-PEOR**, **BAALZEBUB**, or various Greek or Romans gods by some sources.

CHI (key): According to mysticism, the life-giving force of the cosmos, composed of opposites known as Yin and Yang, which flow in all living things and enter the human body through channels known as mediums.

CHILD SACRIFICE: Worship of Moloch included child sacrifice; other instances not specifically related to Moloch-worship are listed in the Old Testament. (Note: Moloch is a god also included in demonology and child sacrifice appears in various books on the occult as it relates to a "Black Mass".) Practiced today throughout the United States by Satanists. Infants are produced through **BREEDERS** within the coven.

CHIROMANCY: Divination from studying the lines of the head.

CHIROGNOMY: The study of the general shape or formation of the hand.

CHRESMOMANCY: Determining the future by the utterances of one in a frenzy.

CHRIST FAMILY: The Christ Family started in the 60's by using transient type people (late teens – early twenties). They (allegedly) harbor runaway kids. Their mission is to let us know that this is the end of times. They wear white sheets, army blankets and have bare feet. Men will wear diapers on their heads for bandannas. They appear to be into transportation of drugs. Vehicles by the Christ Family will have Star of David with lightning bolt through it. If the leader of the group is inside the vehicle, his arch angels will be armed with small caliber handguns and knives. If a single person of Christ Family is found; and he or she is hurt of injured, it is because the group left them behind. They believe anyone hurt is possessed.

CHRISTIAN SCIENCE: A cult founded in 1879 by Mary Baker Eddy, who wrote "Science and Health with Key to the Scriptures" which teaches death is an illusion, God is Divine Mind, and disease can be removed by right thinking.

CHRISTIAN SPIRITUALIST CHURCH: An organization that promotes mediums and spiritists.

CHRIST-CONSCIOUSNESS: The state of being aware, as many great religious leaders supposedly were, that you are Christ, or that you are God.

CHROMOTHERAPY: The belief that certain colors emit rays that seers and clairvoyants see spiritually to determine the condition of the body and soul; therapists may request the person to hold and object of specific color to alleviate an organic disorder.

CHURCH OF SATAN: Headed by occultist Anton LeVey. It encouraged the development of the animal instincts, self-indulgence, and free sexuality; and included in its rituals a satanic "mass". Male and female participants in the ritual wore black robes with the exception of the naked woman who volunteered to be the "altar". Reports indicate the Church ceased functioning in 1975 and has now been replaced by the Temple of Set, headed by Michael Aquino. (Note: Anton LaVey was a former lion tamer and police photographer.)

CHURCH OF THE SATANIC BROTHERHOOD: Founded in 1972 by ex-members of Church of Satan.

CHURCH UNIVERSAL AND TRIUMPHANT: A spiritistic cult founded more than 30 years ago that teaches that spiritual purification is obtained by decreeing that you are God.

CINGULUM: A magickal cord worn around the waist and used for binding, measuring and counting.

CIRCLE: In every level of the occult, the circle represents wholeness. A ritual circle is used to protect conjurers as they stand outside the circle to summon demons; Satanists sometimes proudly insist that they stand within the circle as the demon is summoned for complete possession. Often a group of witches, called a coven, is termed a circle.

CLAIRAUDIENCE: Extrasensory data perceived as sound; generally considered a facet of clairvoyance. Also the ability to hear mentally without using the ears.

CLAIRVOYANCE (SECOND SIGHT): The ability to discern objects or information not present to the normal senses. Mental "seeing" of physical objects oR events at a distance by psychic means. Distinguished from telepathy, which involves ESP.

CLEROMANCY: Casting lots using pebbles or other objects, often of different colors.

COLORS: Colors are symbolic of various meanings. Black: evil, devil, sorrow, darkness; Blue: pornography, sadness, water; Green: nature, soothing, restful, cleansing; Red: blood, sex energy; White: purity, innocence, sincerity; Yellow: power, gory, wealth, perfection; Orange: adaptability, desanctification; Purple: progress, ambition, power.

COLOR DIAGNOSIS AND COLOR THERAPY: We are all aware of the fact that colors can have a helpful or an inhibiting effect on the human psyche. Colors can enliven or depress. Warm colors can warm a person's feelings. Cold colors harden one's sensitivity.

Many color therapists believe that every human body and every organ in it has a certain frequency band of its own. Spiritist mediums can see the frequency band as an *aura*. In case of illness or strong changes of character, the frequency band is altered. These alterations can be detected by a rod and pendulum type apparatus. According to the diagnosis made, the altered frequency is corrected by means of colored threads and bags.

Some people are determined to be deceived by these methods:

> "I went to the color therapist. He told me what was wrong with me by using a pendulum. Then he gave me a small bag containing a colored thread. I was told to wear the bag on the diseased part of

my body and I would be healed."

"The color therapist gave me a large ball of cotton with some colored thread. I was told to wave this cotton ball around my body in circular and straight movements in order to increase the diminished frequency of the diseased organ."

Farmers sometimes use a tin can containing a colored thread which they bury under the cow barn to prevent the cows from calving prematurely or becoming sick.

In connection with color therapy there is all manner of deception and superstition as well as the use of rods, pendulums, and spiritist aura. In short, many forms of occultism are combined

CONCEPTOLOGY/ CONCEPT THERAPY: Claims to sum up the wisdom of the ages concerning man's health and welfare, and explains the underlying principle from which all philosophies, religions, and healing therapies spring. Concept therapy teaches the "laws of life" (4 laws of the body, 12 laws of the mind, 12 laws of the soul, and 7 universal laws). Through the knowledge and practice of these laws of life, A person is said to be able to release the cosmic power residing within and live in harmony with the universe, thereby attaining Heaven on earth – health, prosperity, success, and happiness. Ideas are also a form of energy, according to Conceptology, and a person's imagination can be utilized, through concentration on the desired result, to "create" health and prosperity, as well as to influence or change events. Thoughts and ideas send out vibrations that attract to a person's life the concept or picture held in the mond.

CONSCIOUSNESS REVOLUTION: New Age advocates call for a "consciousness revolution" a new way of looking at and experiencing life. The primary focus of the new consciousness is oneness with God, all mankind, the earth, and with the entire universe.

CONTROL: The spirit that sends messages through a medium in trance.

CONE OF POWER: Imaging a vortex of energy directed toward a goal or person is a common ritual performed in witchcraft.

CONJURATION: Evoking or calling up the spirits to do what one commands them to do. They are confined to a triangle or circle drawn upon the floor. The triangle is a symbol of manifestation and the spirit force is to manifest itself inside the triangle or circle.

CORD: Used in magic and to cinch the waist when wearing robes, usually 9 feet long in cotton, silk, or wool. The color is symbolic of rank or of the ritual performed. (Note: there may be variations when working with self-styled groups.)

CONSCIOUSNESS: mental awareness of present "knowing". New Agers usually refer to consciousness as the awareness or perception of one's "inner self", or of inward awareness of external objects or facts.

CONSECRATING: To make, declare or set apart as sacred.

COSMIC CHRIST: In esoteric schools of thought, the Christ is considered to be a universal spirit or cosmic force. The primary goal of this impersonal spirit or force is to guide the spiritual evolution of mankind.

COSMIC CONSCIOUSNESS: A spiritual and mystical perception that all in the universe is "one". To attain cosmic consciousness is to see the universe as God and God as universe.

COSMIC ENERGY: In metaphysics, an undefined force in the universe by which all living beings have their subsistence, the presence of which ensures health and welfare.

COSMIC HUMANISM: In contrast to normative humanism that sees man as the measure of all things, cosmic humanism sees man as having virtually unlimited potential because of his inner divinity.

CONSULTER WITH FAMILIAR SPIRIT: Consulting the supposed spirits of the dead.

COVEN: A group of witches who gather together to perform ceremonies at Sabbats and Sabbaths. Traditionally, the number of members in a coven has been assumed to total thirteen. The earliest reference to this is the claim of Isobel Gowdie in 1662 that the Auldearne witches had "thirteen persons in each coven".

COVENANT OF THE GODDESS: An international, legally incorporated, ecumenical umbrella organization of Witchcraft covens providing legal corporate status for otherwise unincorporated groups.

COVENATOR: Minister of lowest rank.

COVENDOM: The area within three miles of the Coven's domain.

COVENSTEAD: Place where the coven meets.

COWMAN: One who is not a Witch. Outsider.

CREMATION: The practice of burning the dead body, historically founded on the Eastern mystical concept that unless the body is destroyed, it will be a prison for the soul and prevent future transmigrations (reincarnations).

CRÈME, BENJAMIN: A father of the New age movement and a guiding force through his channeled sessions when he is "overshadowed" by the spirit of Lord Maitreya.

CRESCENT: The shape of the waxing moon, symbolic of fertility and abundant growth.

CRITOMANCY: Observation of barley cakes for possible omens.

CROSS: Ancient pre-Christian symbol interpreted by some occultists as uniting the male phallus (vertical bar) and female vagina (horizontal bar). It is also a symbol of the four directions and a powerful weapon against evil. Not all crosses represent Christianity. The crucifix is not a Christian cross.

CROSS OF NERO: The early 60's peace symbol, an upside down, broken cross in a circle.

CRYONICS: The practice of freezing the body upon death for future thawing and rejuvenation once a cure is found for whatever caused its demise.

CRYSTALS: New age advocates believe that crystals contain incredible healing and energizing powers. Crystals are often touted as being able to restore the "flow of energy" in the human body.

CRYSTAL BALL READING: Determining the future by gazing into a fire.

CRYSTALLOMANCY: Gazing into a crystal ball or other object.

CULT: A religious organization founded by and built upon the teachings of a central charismatic figure whose authority is viewed as being equal to or greater than the Holy Scriptures. In Christian understanding, the teachings of a cult oppose or differ from historic biblical theology.

CURSE: Invocation of an oath associated with black magic or sorcery intended to harm or destroy opponents or property; curses often require the invocation of evil spirits.

CURSES OR SPELLS - Curses or the casting or breaking of spells. Curses may be incurred as a result of our sins or the sins of our forefathers (Deuteronomy 27 & 28). Spells are produced by occult practitioners by the release of demonic power through hypnosis, magnetism, mesmerism, or some other form of magic resulting in extrasensory influence. Spells stir up love or hate, persecute or defend against enemies, kill humans or animals, and heal or inflict diseases.

CYCLOMANCY: Divination from a turning wheel.

D

DACTYLMANCY: A dangling ring indicates words and numbers by its swings.

DAEMON: From the Greek, Diamon: A spirit, an evil spirit or demon. Also used as a term for beings at an intermediate level between God and people.

DAGON: The national god of the Philistines.

DAIMON (DAIMONIAN): A demon, signified among pagan Greeks as an inferior deity.

DAIMONIODAS: A Greek word meaning "from the devil" or "of the devil".

DAIMONIZOMAI: A Greek work that means "demonized", although unfortunately it is usually translated "demon-possessed". "Daimonizomai" can usually refer to a wide range of demonic influence.

DAPHNOMANCY: Listening to branches, particularly laurel branches, burning in a fire; the louder the crackle, the better the omen.

"DARK SIDE OF THE MOON": A popular album by a rock group Pink Floyd featuring spacey sounds and musically adventuresome elements that have inspired some New Age musicians; believed by some to facilitate mind expansion techniques.

DEATH METAL MUSIC: Themes include Satanism, torture, murder, rape, suicide, self-mutilation, anti-Christian. Some groups that play death metal music include "Mayhem," "Slayer," and "Deicide."

"DECLARATION OF INTERDEPENDENCE": A globalist document, drafted by the World Affairs Council in 1975, representing the New Age agenda by stating the world cannot survive unless mankind recognized "the necessity for collaborative regulation by international authorities".

DECREES: Oral affirmations invoking supernatural powers by the authority of the words spoken, similar to chanting a mantra.

DÉJÀ VU: The feeling of having already experienced an event or place that is being encountered for the very first time.

DEMON: A non-human spirit; generally thought by many theologians to be disembodied spirits from a pre-adamic earth, as differentiated from fallen angels.

DEMONCRACY: Worship of an evil nature.

DEMONIZATION (DEMONIZED) – Demonization occurs when an evil spirit or spirits inhabit a person's soul. Usually as a result of sin, generational curses, or severe trauma. *See Appendix J*

DEMONOLOGY: The study of demons, what they are designated to do and how they are summoned, as well as what role they play with mankind today.

DENDROMANCY: Divination utilizing oak or mistletoe.

DENTROLATRY: Worship of trees.

DERASH: A Hebrew word for "one that inquires of the dead".

DEVIL: The personification of evil called Lucifer or Satan. The word means accuser or slanderer.

DHARMA: Law, truth, or teaching; used to express the central teaching of Hindu and Buddhist religion. Dharma implies that essential truth can be stated about the way things are, and that people could comply with that norm.

DIABLERIE: Dealing with demons or the Devil; sorcery or witchcraft.

DIABOLUS: Two morsels, kill body and soul.

DIAKKA: Spirits that communicate with or materialize for mediums or spiritists.

DIANA: Greek fertility goddess, also known in other eras as Aphrodite, Ashtoreth, or Artemis, venerated by those New Agers who believe in the resacralization of the earth.

DIANETICS: Ron Hubbard's teaching on mental health.

DIRECTIONS, FOUR: In Western magic, the four directions are symbolized in ritual, representing the elements air, fire, water and earth, respectively.

DISASSOCIATION: Avoiding pain or unpleasantness by redefining reality with other mental associations, such as thinking that firewalking coals are cool moss.

DISCARNATE: The soul or personality of a living creature who has died.

DISCIPLE: Lay member.

DIVINATION: Methods of discovering the personal, human significance of present or future events. Means to obtain insights may include dreams, hunches, involuntary body actions, mediumistic possession, consulting the dead, observing the behavior of animals and birds, tossing coins, casting lots, and "reading" natural phenomena.

DIVINER'S STAFF: Refers to a staff used for divination.

DIVINING ROD - A forked object (hazel tree twig, wire, etc.) used to locate water (water witching) minerals or other objects. Evil spirits actually locate the water or other objects and move the divining rod.

DOWSING (DOWSER): (Also Water Diviner) A person skilled in locating underground sources of water by means of a divining rod. The dowser uses a Y-shaped rod that is generally made of hazel, but is sometimes made of metal or substitute woods like rowan or ash. As the dowser walks above the location of the underground water, the rod jerks in an involuntary and spontaneous manner, indicating to the dowser both the location and the depth of the supply. Unknown to the dowser he is working hand in hand with evil spirits and ultimately there is a "pay back" for this knowledge to the dowser's detriment.

DRAGON: In Revelation 20:2, Satan is identified as "the dragon".

DRAWING DOWN THE MOON: A Wiccan rite of invoking the Moon Goddess. A book by Margot Adler about Neo-Pagan religious movement, widely regarded as the best study of Neo-Paganism ever written.

DREAM CATCHERS: A charm thought to possess occult power.   The dream catcher may be very popular but it is not an innocent ornament.   It is actually a charm.   A charm is "any magic word, formula, incantation, object, sign or amulet supposed to possess occult power."[1]

One witchcraft magazine, in an article titled "Amulets, Talismans & Charms," explains the dream catcher like this:

> *This charm, from the Ojibway tribe in Minnesota, is made of sinew stretched over a small hoop of ash.   It is designed to bring a good night's sleep, especially for children, and is hung horizontally over a child's cradleboard or crib.   Tradition says that the air is filled with both good and bad dreams waiting to come to a sleeping child.   This net allows good dreams to find their way to the child through the hole in the center, while bad dreams are caught up in the web where they dissolve in the dawn's light.   Dream nets continue to be used by some Ojibway people today as in ancient times.[2]*

One paper explaining the *"Legend of the Dream Catcher"* states:

> *Long ago when the world was young, an old Lakota spiritual leader was on a high mountain and had a vision.   In his vision, Iktomi, the great trickster and teacher of wisdom, appeared in the form of a spider.   Iktomi spoke to him in a sacred language that only the spiritual leaders of the Lakota could understand... All the while the spider spoke, he continued to weave his web starting from the outside and working towards the center... If you believe in the great spirit, the web will catch your good ideas – and the bad ones will go through the hole.   The Lakota elder passed on his vision to his people and now the Sioux Indians use the dream catcher as the web of their life.   It is hung above their beds or in their home to sift their dreams and visions.   The good in their dreams are captured in the web of life and carried with them... but the evil in their dreams escapes through the hole in the center of the web and are no longer a part of them.   They believe that the dream catcher holds the destiny of their future.[3]*

The spider (Iktomi) was known as a trickster.   How can you be sure that he didn't trick the people with his tale of the dream catcher?   How can you be sure that the good dreams are caught and the evil ones are filtered out?   A trickster is known for lying, deception, and mischief.

---

[1] Frank Gaynor, Editor, *Dictionary of Mysticism*, New York: Philosophical Library, 1953, p. 35

[2] Selena Fox, *Amulets, Talismans & Charms: Past and Present*, Circle Network News, Summer 1987, Vol. 9, No. 2, p. 13.

[3] Paper entitled *"Legend of the Dream Catcher."*

Most Christians researchers will recognize the occultic connotations expressed in this story. The fantasy of a spider speaking, the use of visions, the "sacred language," and the idea that it is the dream catcher that holds each person's destiny rather than God.

Another catalog that sells lots of occultic materials states:

> **THE DREAM CATCHER WEB**. Believe in its <u>mystical powers</u>, and you may sleep more peacefully! Through the center <u>spirit</u> hole flow your good dreams; trapped in the web are the "bad," which disappear with the morning sun.[4] *(underlining added)*

You may have noticed even the descriptions of the dream catcher differ from place to place. Some people believe that the bad dreams are caught in the web and others believe that the good dreams are caught. Regardless of the discrepancies, this is not an item that any Christian would want in their home.

DREAM THERAPY: The theory that future events can be determined by dream analysis since these visions supposedly reveal the goal and desires of one's higher spiritual self.

DRUIDS: Celtic priests in pre-Christian Britain and Gaul. Skilled in astronomy and medicine, they worshiped the sun, believed in the immortality of the soul, and in reincarnation. Very powerful and very dangerous – still active today.

DRYAD: A tree spirit, generally seen as feminine.

DUALISM: The doctrine that for every principle there is an opposing, separate, and ultimately irreconcilable counter-principle. Such opposing forces are conventionally arrayed along a good-evil dichotomy.

DUNGEONS AND DRAGONS: A fantasy role-playing game which uses demonology, witchcraft, voodoo, murder, rape, blasphemy, suicide, assassination, insanity, sex perversion, homosexuality, prostitution, Satan type rituals, gambling, barbarism, cannibalism, sadism, desecration, demon summoning, necromantics, divination and many other teachings. There have been a number of deaths nationwide where games like Dungeons & Dragons were either the decisive factor in adolescent suicide and murder, or played a major factor in the violent behavior in such tragedies. Since role-playing is used typically for behavior modification, it has

---

[4] Catalog from Red Rose Collection, Holiday 1992, p. 46

become apparent nationwide (with the increased homicide and suicide rates in adolescents) that there is a great need to investigate every aspect of the youngster's environment, including their method of entertainment, in reaching a responsible conclusion for their violent actions.

E

EAR ACUPUNCTURE: A form of auricular therapy based on the concept that the ear is shaped like a fetus-in-utero and is a microcosm that contains reference points by which the body can supposedly be affected.

EARTH LOGOS: Some New Age advocates believe that the Earth Logos is a great spiritual being who is the ensouling life of planet earth. The earth is considered a physical manifestation (or body) of this spiritual intelligence.

EARTH-MOTHER: Female personification of the Lifeforce, fertility of the Earth and its inhabitants. One of the most widespread deity concepts in the world. (Peib) The ancient Greeks called her Gaia, and equated her with both Mother Earth and Mother Nature.

EASTERN RELIGIONS - Any involvement in Hinduism, Confucianism, Buddhism, Taoism, Shintoism, Islam (Muslim).

EAST WEST: Monthly New Age magazine accentuating occult, mystical, and natural healing methods, along with metaphysical nutrition.

ECOSOPHY: Greek, "wisdom of the home." A holistic, pantheistic, metaphysical world-view based on emergent evolution, imminent divinity, and the Gaeia Thesis.

ECTOPLASM: A white filmy substance pouring from a medium's bodily openings, supposedly denoting the presence of a disembodied spirit, or a sticky, milky-white substance out of which poltergeists and discarnate (disembodied) entities are said to materialize for the purpose of visible manifestation.

EDGAR CAYCE: A minister involved in "channeling" who provided "cures" for many sick persons. There are many books by and about him.

EIDOLEION: A worshiper of idols.

EIDOLOLATREIA: Something that is sacrificed to an idol.

EIDOLON: An idol.

EIDOLOTHUTON: Something that is sacrificed to an idol.

EIKON: An image, in Revelation 13, an image of the beast is made, which people are required to worship.

EL: A generic name for a god or gods; also used of God.

ELAEOMANCY: Divination by observation of a liquid surface.

ELAH: God, or a god; an object of worship used by pagans in reference to their various duties.

ELDER GODS: Gods that occasionally come to rescue men from the "Ancient Ones".

ELECTROMAGNETIC HEALING: The theory that an electrical force animates the body, and that its proper stabilization contributes to health and healing.

ELEMENTAL: A familiar, or one of the four classes of demons.

ELEMENTS: The early Greeks considered Earth, Air, Fire and Water to be the four elements.

ELF FIRE: Fire produced without the aid of metals, used to light a balefire.

ELIL: Literally an empty or vain, worthless thing.

ELIZEN (ELTZEN): Ruler of the spirits of the North.

ELVES: From Norse "Aelfar". Originally the Tuatha de Danaan (Children of the Goddess Danu); early bronze-age Celts, also known as the Sidhe. Later mythologized and amalgamated with **FAIRIES**.

EMAH: Idols that impress terror on their worshipers.

ENCHANTER: Sorcerer, magician, one who uses human voice or music to bring another person into psychic control. Lev. 19:26; Deut. 18:10-12; II Chron. 33:6; II Kings 17:17; Is. 47:9,11; Jer. 27:9; Dan. 1:20.

ENCHANTMENT: The act of influencing by charms and incantations the practice of magical arts.

ENOCH: According to Genesis, Enoch was a man who "walked with God" and was taken to heaven without suffering death; occultists attribute various special powers and abilities to him.

ENLIGHTENMENT: The realization that you are God (akin to self-actualization). A state of awareness (sometimes called "nirvana," "cosmic consciousness," or "transcendental bliss") that assumes all of existence is interwoven and man is innately god with untapped potential.

ENTROPY: Degradation of the matter and energy in the universe to an ultimate state of inert uniformity (see *Syntropy*, entropy's opposite).

EQUINOX: The time at which the sun crossed the equator. The equinox takes place on March 21 and September 22, and on these days the length of the day and night are equal.

EQUIVALENCY: A socialist concept that insists no nation should have an overabundance of resources, that commerce and substance should be distributed equivalently.

EREBUS: According to Greek mythology, a dark region through which souls traveled on their way to Hades.

ERHERD, WERNER: Founder of "est", a mind-expansion cult that teaches reality can be intuitively experienced because "being" is more important than "doing".

ESALEN INSTITUTE: A "growth" center that offers a wide variety of workshops for mind, body and spirit. It is located in Big Sur, California.

ESBAT: Coven meetings held on a regular basis usually at least once a month at the full moon. It is at these meetings "work" is performed such as healing and "magick".

ESOTERIC: Term applied to teachings that are secret and only for initiate of the group; mysterious, occult, "hidden". A word used to describe knowledge that is possessed or understood only by a few.

ESOTERIC CHRISTIANITY: A mystical form of Christianity that sees its "core truth" as identical to the "core truth" of every other religion (i.e. Man is divine). This form of Christianity is at home with Aldous Huxley's "perennial philosophy". (See: Perennial Philosophy)

ESOTERIC DOCTRINE: Occultists claim that there exists mystical teaching known to the most highly evolved adepts, parts of which can be found in various religions, but is wholly contained in no single one; this doctrine is presumably given by seers to the world in times of great need.

ESOTERIC PHILOSOPHY: The study of secret knowledge understood by and revealed to only a select few initiates, who usually attain such information by spirit guides or arcane, sacred books.

ESP (EXTRASENSORY PERCEPTION): The experience of, or response to, an external event, object, state, or influence without apparent contact through the known sense. ESP may occur without those being aware of it. Short for "extrasensory perception", the psychic ability to perceive things intuitively beyond the capability of the five natural senses; paranormal abilities such as telepathy, precognition and clairvoyance.

ESP CARDS: A pack of twenty-five cards bearing five symbols, including stars, squares, circles, crosses and waves.

EST: Acronym for **ERHARD SEMINARS TRAINING**, a process of getting "it" by intuitive acquisition after long hours of deprivation and verbal humiliation. Name has since been changed to The Forum.

ETSEB (ATSAR, OSTEB): A Hebrew word for an idol whose service is laborious or is cause of grief.

EVERQUEST: Everquest is a computer role-playing game requiring an Internet connection and a paid monthly membership. The packaging notes state there is animated blood and gore, animated violence, and suggestive themes. The back of the game box this author checked states "Hundreds of new magical items to discover, trade and sell."

In the Everquest series there is violence that involves the use of axes and swords to kill, the casting of spells and throwing curses to kill opposing members, and a classic cyber world where nobody will stop you from killing other players. The chat feature allows the player to communicate with his team and opponents often resulting in sexual harassment between players, cyber stalking, and profanity.

Magick and the occult are numerous. The player must acquire magic skills to have a chance of winning. For many players the "quest" is to attain more and more magical power and use it on those in the real world.

Included are generous amounts of nearly naked female characters. Young boys and men are being exposed to barely-dressed women at every turn and fighting and killing them when given a chance. Psychologists warn about mixing sex and violence, especially with impressionable young ones.

With the interactive chat going on between players, not only is there much profanity and sexual harassment, but the chat rooms can be entered by adult predators to converse with children. Children already pumped up by the sexy violence flooding the screen.

Everquest needs to be avoided for its violence, occultism, mature content, and chat room dangers.

EVIL EYE: A superstition which credits certain people with the ability to dispense bad luck with a gaze; people hope to counteract by wearing charms or amulets.

EXORCISM: The act of removing demonic control from someone who is demonized; in witchcraft, purifying something from alien influences.

EXOTERIC CHRISTIANITY: A form of Christianity identified with historic or orthodox Christianity that New Agers would describe as being devoid of all spiritual authenticity.

EYES: The "evil eye" is feared.

F

FAIRIES: From the pre-Celtic past, fairies are also known as Goblins and are classified with Leprechauns, Brownies, and Pixies. They stand for the evil spirits that were once thought at the Vigil of Samhain and the Eve of Halloween. Fairies were believed to be able to predict death. They were also known as little people who created problems for the Celtics.

FALLEN ANGELS: Angels deceived by Lucifer into believing he was the anointed one, the true Son of God. These angels were cast out of heaven with Lucifer and are among the unknown number of evil spirits today.

FAMILIAR SPIRIT: A demonic spirit who serves a witch or medium, or an animal that it may inhabit.

FAM-TRAD: Family tradition. Psychic training and/or magickal traditions identified with Witchcraft and handed down as hereditary or family lore.

FASCINATION: The act of charming or casting a spell on someone nearby by a projection of power through the eye, etc.

FAUN: A minor Roman spirit of the wilderness. Humanoid, but with goat's horns, legs, hooves and tail. May be male or female.

FAUNUS: Brother/lover of Fauna. The "Red Man". Male collective spirit of the animal kingdom.

FELDENKRAIS: System of bodywork founded by Moshe Feldenkrais, teaching that emotional and spiritual balance is achieved through functional coordination, body awareness, and stipulated movements.

FERGUSON, MARILYN: Prominent New Age theorist and author of the movement's classic "The Aquarian Conspiracy".

FETISH: An inanimate object presumably inhabited by a spirit.

FINDHORN COMMUNITY: A legendary New Age community located in the North of Scotland. The group offers an ongoing educational program in the principles of New Age spirituality.

FINGER: Holds spiritual powers. Index finger is known as "poison, witch or cursing finger". Many believe you must not use it to touch a wound or it will never heal.

FIRE: Symbolizes Satan.

FIREWALKING: Supernatural ability to walk over hot coals without feeling pain. An ancient, idolatrous ritual in which one seeks spiritual purification by walking on super-heated coals to prove one's confidence in the god's protection.

FLORAMANCY: Determining the future by study of flowers.

FLOTATION TANKS: Cylinders containing a saline solution in which people lie, floating on the water's surface (often in darkness) to create the illusion of cosmic awareness to achieve spiritual enlightenment.

FORCE, THE: A concept presented by George Lucas in the "Star Wars" movie epics; based on the Taoist idea of a primordial essence that is both good and evil and may be used for either, depending on one's motive.

FORTUNE TELLING: The art of forecasting future events and reading human character. Foretelling the future in other peoples' lives, usually with the aid of the spirit world, or with aid of some "spirit" aide.

FREEMASONRY: *See Appendix A*

FREYA: Scandinavian Goddess of Love, Queen of Lower Regions. Freya's sacred day was Friday. Witches held weekly assemblies on Friday.

FULL MOON: Greatest magical power.

G

GAIA: A Greek name for the goddess of the earth. It also refers to a scientific hypothesis formulated by James Lovelock whereby all living matter on the earth is believed to be a single living organism. In such a scheme, humanity is considered the nervous system of the living earth.

GARDNER, GERALD: (1884-1964) Founder of modern Witchcraft, author of Witchcraft Today (1954) and other books. Gardnerian Wicca remains his legacy.

GARDNERIAN WITCHCRAFT: Traditional witchcraft system founded by Gerald Gardner in England.

GASTROMANCY: An ancient form of ventriloquism; prophetic utterances were delivered in this way.

GELOSCOPY: Divination from the tone of someone's laughter.

GENETHLIALOGY: Observation of the position and influence of the stars at a person's birth to predict their future.

GEOMANCY: Interpretation of figures or dots drawn on the ground, or perhaps on paper, according to accepted designs.

GHOSTS: Thought by some to be spirit apparitions through which the souls of dead persons are thought to manifest themselves. To others, a ghost is a demon spirit which has been unleashed by Satan to live in a certain environment. Some explain ghosts away by attributing strange happenings to natural causes.

GLOBALISM: A modern-day term referring to the need for transformation from the present nation-state divisions into a one world community.

GLORY DUST: See *Golden Glory.*

GNOME: An elemental who lives in the earth.

GNOSTICISM: Refers to the secret doctrines and practices of mysticism whereby a person may come to enlightenment or realization that he or she is of the same essence of God or the Absolute. The Greek word Gnosis means knowledge, and at the heart of Gnostic thought is the idea that revelation of the hidden gnosis frees one from the fragmentary and illusory material world and teaches him or her about the origins of the spiritual world, to which the Gnostic belongs by nature.

GOAT: Occultist believe Satan appears in the form of a goat.

GOAT'S HEAD: Sixteenth century symbol for Satan. (Note: This appears to still hold true in present practices.)

GOAT OF MENDES: A satanic symbol, the opposite of the Lamb of God (Jesus).

GOD: The New Age god is referred to as a "universal consciousness," "universal life," or "universal energy," an impersonal force that pervades the universe. A being who has "many faces." He (it) is considered a radically imminent being who is often referred to as a "universal consciousness," "universal life," or "universal energy". The New Age god is more or less an impersonal force that pervades the universe.

GOETIA: Tradition of black magic, including incantations, ceremonies, and techniques of sorcery, often providing practical instructions for contacting demonic spirits. (Note: Also known as the lesser key of Solomon.)

GOLDEN DAWN, ORDER OF THE: Ceremonial magickal lodge founded in 1887 by a trio of English Freemasons. Its prominent members included S.L. MacGregor

Mathers, W.B. Yeats, Israel Regardie, Dion Forutne, A.E. Waite, and Aleister Crowley, who was eventually expelled. Its purpose was "to prosecute the Great Work: which is to obtain control of the nature and power of my own being."

GOLDEN GLORY: A demonically inspired activity thought by some to be the visible presence of God, the same glory that was seen on the face of Moses when he came down from the mountain of God. It appears as gold flakes that come through the pores of the skin on the face or hands or some other part of the body. Some say their fillings turn to gold. Others have experienced it raining down from heaven, falling on either people, their clothing, or their surroundings. The deception effects every denomination and has been experienced worldwide. This author has witnessed its manifestation with clients while counseling but when tested an evil spirit manifests.

GRAPHOLOGY: A psychic analysis of someone's handwriting. See *handwriting analysis.*

GREAT BEAST: The name for the Anti-Christ in the Book of Revelation, and the name popularly associated with the magician Aleister Crowley.

GREAT INVOCATION: A New Age prayer that has been translated into over 80 languages; to invoke the presence of the cosmic Christ, leading to the oneness of all mankind.

GREAT RITE: Ritual sex within the magick circle.

GREEN MAGIC: Used for working with vegetation, as in gardening. Fertility and prosperity.

GRIMOURES: A medieval collection of magical spells, rituals, incantations. Also any coven or circle's book of shadows recording spells, ceremonies and history of the group.

GRIS-GRIS ("Grey-grey"): Medicine power sometimes in the form of herbal pouches. Used in New Orleans Cajun-style "Voodoo."

GROTTO: A Satanic congregation.

GROUP GURU: A slang New Age term referring to the idea that the Cosmic Christ is incarnate in all of humanity. All mankind is seen as a single "guru".

GROVES: A group of covens potentially many who will form regional and national conferences.

GURU: Spiritual teacher who instructs disciples in the "way" of enlightenment. The guru's authority is to be implicitly accepted.

GYROMANCY: Use of a person spinning in a circle and then falling to the ground to determine the future.

H

HAIR: Holds character. In witch hunt times, it was believed a sorcerer's magical potency was in his hair.

HALLOWEEN - A November Eve witches' holiday; considered to be the day of the year most suitable for magic or demonic activity. (Oct. 31, also believed to be the time when the souls of the deceased revisited their former homes and once again enjoyed the company of their kinfolk.) See *Appendix B.*

HAND OF DEATH: A cult which allegedly sacrifices people and has rituals that are Satanic. They are allegedly into cannibalism. Lucus and Toole allegedly were part of this group. Very little is known about this group.

HAND OF GLORY: The left hand of a person who has died. The hand is removed and a candle is positioned between the fingers. The ritual is used for protection against evil spirits.

HANDWRITING ANALYSIS: also known as graphology is a form of divination falling in a category similar to palm reading whereby such things as an individual's character, career potential, trustworthiness, emotional development, personality, and other hidden characteristics are said to be revealed through an analysis of his handwriting.

HARMONIC CONVERGENCE: The assembly of New Age mediators gathered at the same astrological time in different locations to usher in peace on earth and one-world government.

HARRY POTTER: See *Appendix E*

HAURSCOPY (HEIROMANCY, HUROSCOPY): Various names for observation of cuts, cracks, or markings in very old objects and drawing prophetic conclusions.

HEAD: Central powerhouse of the body believed to contain all magical powers. For this reason many human skulls are used on altars. Also, eating of the brain is believed to transfer power.

HEALING FANATICISM: Involvement in "faith healing" cults or with "faith healers" who are involved in sensationalism.

HEALING MAGIC: See Magic: Healing.

HEART: The symbol of eternity. Some groups believe that by eating the heart of another, you acquire the characteristics of the victim and obtain all of his power. The heart is symbolic of the center of life.

HEAVY METAL ROCK: "Heavy metal cultivates a macho image with black leather chains and spikes or studs attached to leather wrist bands, belts and jackets. When you think of heavy metal, you think of power. Women are sometimes portrayed in degrading situations. Heavy-Metal album covers and videos sometimes show women being dragged around by the hair, caged or being walked on a leash like dogs. The main focus of the heavy metaler is drugs, sex and rock'n'roll. The most alarming aspect of heavy metal is its preoccupation with the occult. There's some subtle and not so subtle Satanic overtones in Heavy Metal. Album covers include such things as illustrations of devil's heads, crucified figures, demonic babies, skeletons, pentagrams, black candles and the occult number 666". (Quotes by Darlyne Pettinichio, Probation Officer from Orange County, Calif., News Article, the Press Enterprise, Riverside, Ca., May 7, 1986.) The six themes of Heavy Metal Music are: the death of God; sex with corpses; human sacrifices; sitting at Satan's left hand; calling Jesus Christ the deceiver; and glorifying the name of Satan.

HECATE: Goddess of Lower Regions and Patroness of Witchcraft.

HECHICERIA: The surviving remnants of true Native Indian magical religion in Mexico. Practitioners are most often male and are called hechiceros, or naguals (in Nahuatl), or sometimes even bruho naturaleza. They believe that those born to be hechiceros are called by the gods from a hereditary line. They worship the old pre-Columbian divinities with fragments of surviving rites and indigenous folk rituals.

HELLFIRE CLUBS: During the 18th and 19th centuries, these small groups in Europe reintroduced the Black Mass and other satanic practices, including sexual immorality.

HERBOLOGY: Use of plants as natural healing substances to promote health and cure minor illnesses.

HERMETIC TRADITIONS: Occult teachings that arose during the first three centuries A.D.

HEXAGRAM: A six-point talismatic star, also known as a Star of David. The Hexagram is believed among occultists to protect and control demons.

HIGHER SELF: The most "spiritual" and "knowing" part of oneself, said to lie beyond the ego, the day-to-day personality, and the personal unconscious. The Higher Self can supposedly be channeled for wisdom and guidance. Variations include the Oversoul, the Superconsciousness, the Atman, the Christ (or Krishna or Buddha) Consciousness, and the god Within.

HINDUISM: Dominant religion of the Indian subcontinent; teaches that God is impersonal and unknowable and that man's ultimate purpose, after the effect of bad deeds has been dissipated, is to re-emerge into the oneness of the inexplicable.

HIPPOMANCY: Divination from the neighing and stamping of horses.

HOLISM: A unitary philosophy that claims organic or environmental systems consist of similar parts, integrated as a whole. The theory that all reality is organically one. Everything in the universe is viewed as interrelated and interdependent.

HOLISTIC: Alternatively, but less frequently, spelled "wholistic"; derived from the Greek holos, meaning "whole" in the sense of "entire" or "unified". Holistic health practices emphasize the whole person, the impact of the environment, and the interdependence of all parts of the body, mind, and spirit in the prevention and treatment of ailments.

HOLISTIC HEALTH: Sees the person as an interrelated organism; needing to be treated as a whole person (body, mind and spirit), as opposed to merely treating a particular disease.

HOLOGRAM: A three-dimensional projection resulting from the interaction of laser beams. Scientists have discovered that the image of an entire hologram can be reproduced from any one of its many component parts. New Agers use this to illustrate the oneness of all reality.

HOMEOPATHY: A "natural" way of stimulating the body's healing ability by using the theory that "like cures like", which treats patients with the same substance that sickened them.

HOODOO: A combination of black magic and Voodoo used only to bring bad luck.

HORNED GOD: Symbol of male sexuality in paganism and witchcraft; part man, part goat.

HOROSCROPE: A chart showing a person's destiny as determined by astrology practice.

HOUSES: The 12 sections of the Zodiac which together symbolize every aspect of life. The planets move through the houses; thus, when a planet falls into the sphere of the given house, it comes under its respective influence. The astrologer plots all of these factors and more on a chart. This chart is called a horoscope.

HUBBARD, L. RON: Science fiction writer (1911-1986) and founder of the Scientology cult, which believes humanity descended from an extraterrestrial race of omnipotent gods known as Thetans; also wrote on "Dianetics".

HUMAN POTENTIAL MOVEMENT: A movement with roots in humanistic psychology that stresses man's essential goodness and unlimited potential; the answer is seen to be "within".

HUMANISM: A doctrine that supposes mankind is the ultimate essence of worth, and no divine being exists to determine the ideals and values of humanity. A system of philosophy that upholds the primacy of human beings rather than God or any abstract or metaphysical system. Humanism holds that man is the measure of all things.

HYDROMANCY: Observing any number of several aspects of water, including its color, ebb and flow, or ripples caused by pebbles dropped into a pool.

HYPERVENTILATION: Based on the Hindu theory that biocosmic power is in the breath and that by rapid breathing, one may transcend to a state of spiritual awareness.

HYPNOSIS: State resembling deep sleep or trance, but more active in that the person has some will and feeling but acts according to suggestions presented; a heightened sense of suggestibility to the imagination.

HYPNOTHERAPY: A psychological therapy which involves the use of hypnosis.

HYPNOTIC REGRESSION: The process by which one is said to recall past-life memories through hypnosis.

HYPNOTISM - Being Hypnotized by anyone (individually or in a group) for any purpose.

I

I-CHING: Chinese book of divination associated with Taoism. I-Ching consists of the *Book of Changes*, written by Chinese mystics, which gives the interpretation of marked yarrow sticks that are cast by the person desiring information about something. The *Book of Changes* contains mystic sayings, abstract principles, symbolic concepts and explanations which form the basis for divination. The yarrow sticks are tossed (some use coins or special cards) and their pattern is used as a guide in consulting the "Wisdom" of the *Book of Changes* in order to find the answers to a person's questions, or to receive the guidance needed. The system is based upon numerous hexagrams (six-line figures) which reveal what the *Book of Changes* have to say.

ICONS: Sacred ornate frames decorated with images of Christ or Saints.

IDOLATRY: Worship of an idol.

IMMANENT DIVINITY: The theological position that Nature includes Divinity; that Divinity is a quality, not a quantity, and may be found within, not without.

IMMORTALITY: Immunity from any kind of death or decay that comes from having eternal, divine life; in Christianity, that immortality is received from God as his gracious gift as we believe on the Lord Jesus Christ and are saved.

INCANTATIONS: Repetitive use of words, phrases or sounds to produce a magical effect. Verbal spells recited by a practitioner in an effort to summon evil forces.

INCENSE: Any of various substances, such as hums, resins or herbs, producing a pleasant odor when burned and used in religious ceremonies for purifications and offerings.

INCUBI (INCUBUS): An evil spirit in male form sent for sexual purposes, usually with a human female. The victim feels weight and penetration but usually sees nothing. Throughout history there have been instances of women and men who were sexually assaulted or molested by some entity, usually invisible, believed to be either an evil spirit, the spirit form of a deceased person, or the astral body of a sorcerer or sorceress. The incubus is a male entity which assaults women for the purpose of gratifying its sexual appetite, and the succubus is its female counterpart which preys on men for this purpose.

These experiences cannot be dismissed as merely "sexual dreams," "hallucinations," or "hysterical delusions" by psychotic individuals, for such instances are generally reported by normal, rational persons, including Christians. Such bizarre assaults by demons and other spirit entities have long been investigated and reported by the church, as well as by other investigators.

Actual case histories are recorded by contemporary ministers, psychologists, and psychiatrists, including this writer. It is common knowledge that there are numerous instances reported by witches and mediums concerning their sexual relations with demon lovers. Some individuals actually prefer their spirit lovers to normal relations with mortal men and women. The spirits are usually invisible and even so the victims report that the entity has form and weight which can be felt, and that their method of sexual assault is precisely that of a human being.

INITIATE: One who has successfully passed through a ritual of initiation. Also, one who possesses secret knowledge.

INSTITUTE OF NOETIC SCIENCES: A tax-exempt, nonprofit foundation started in 1973 to broaden knowledge of the potentials of mind and consciousness by exploring exceptional abilities, health and healing, and societal transformation.

INTUITION: Ability of knowing, or the knowledge obtained, without conscious recourse to inference or reasoning.

INVERTED CROSS: Upside down cross often seen at occult sites. A mockery of the Christian Cross.

INVERTED PENTAGRAM: Five pointed star with single point downward.

INVOCATION: Calling power in general or calling an evil spirit.

I.P. MESSENGER: Minister of lowest rank.

IPSISSMUS: Highest order held in Satanism. Rarely attainable during a lifetime.

IRIDOLOGY OR IRIS DIAGNOSIS: Receiving treatment for an ailment, from a person not having formal medical training, which is based on the recognition or distinction of diseases by observation of the iris or rainbow membrane of your eye.

ISIS: Egyptian Goddess; Mother Mature; Queen of Heaven; wife of Osiris, mother or Horus. Isis was adopted by Greeks and Romans, and became the most widely-worshiped deity of the Mediterranean world.

ISOLATION TANKS: Alternately referred to as isolation tanks and flotation tanks, these sensory deprivation devices place the patient in a weightless state, sequestered from the outside world. Water laced with Epsom salts creates buoyancy for the purposes of psychic exploration or simple relaxation. The idea is to shut down the conscious mind and enter a state of "samadhi," deep contemplation. A dark, womb-like ambience reduces all sensory input so the patient can enter a natural infantile state.

J

JEAN DIXON - Reading her predictions or belief in her ability to foretell the future. See PRECOGNITION.

JESUS: (In New Age), an avatar who attained a high level of attunement to the Cosmic Christ. This enabled him to become a bodily vehicle for the Christ for a period of three years.

HIN SHIN JYTSU: A Japanese occult healing discipline involving body manipulation at specified points; similar to acupressure.

JUNG, CARL: A disciple of Sigmund Freud who entertained the various forms of occultism, including the idea that the ultimate reality of existence and the source of all truth lies in a "collective unconsciousness" into which spiritually developed beings can tap.

K

KABALA (CABALA): System of Jewish occult mysticism developed by certain rabbis, especially during the Middle Ages, relying heavily on mathematical interpretation of Scripture.

KAHUNA: A native Hawaiian shaman.

KALI: This word means black. Kali is a Hindu goddess who would accept only blood sacrifices. Such sacrifices still are being offered to the goddess today.

KARMA: The law of cause and effect which says that for every action (in this life) there is a reaction (in the next life). What we sow in this life we will reap in the next life.

KARMIC LAW OF JUSTICE: The idea that one's accumulated good and evil deeds will culminate in a fate commensurate with past spiritual accomplishments.

KASHAPH (KESHAPHIM): To practice magic or use incantations, usually with the intent to deceive, pervert, or do mischief; "KASHAPH" refers to the person and "KESHAPHIM" refers to the magical practice.

KATEIDOLOS: Full of idols.

KEMARIM: Idolatrous priests.

KEPPEN ROD: Magical wand used in various ritualistic ceremonies.

KEY OF SOLOMON: Probably the most famous grimoire ever written; some legends hold that it was written by demons and hidden under Solomon's throne. Various versions in different languages survive today.

KIRILIAN: A type of high-voltage photography that uses a pulsed, high-frequency electrical field and two electrodes, between which are placed the object to be photographed and an unexposed film plate. The image captured is purported to be an aura of energy that emanates from plants, animals, and humans an changes in accordance with the physiological or emotional shifts.

KINESIOLOGY: Study of the principles of mechanics and anatomy in relation to human movement.

KNIGHT, J.Z.: Middle-aged housewife who claims to be the "channel" for the entity known as Ramtha, an evil spirit.

KREIGER, DELORES: Originator and popularizer of the therapeutic touch theory.

KRIS: Magic knife of the Malaysians.

KRISHNA: 8th incarnation and avatar of Vishnu, the Preserver god. He has been the most celebrated and revered of all Hindu gods for over 2,000 years.

KRONE TRAINING: New Age motivational teachings, developed by Krone, that critics say are based on the occult teaching of the Armenian mystic Gurdjieff.

KUNDALINI: Psycho-spiritual power thought by yogi(s) to lie dormant at the base of the spine. Believed to be a goddess, Kundalini is referred to as "the serpent power".

L

LADY: Female leader of a coven.

LAMMAS: August witch celebration (August 1, Great Sabbat)

LAMPODEMANCY: Observing lights or torches for omens.

LAVEY, ANTON: American Satanist of Romanian-German-Gypsy parentage, who was the founder and head of the Church of Satan in San Francisco, Calif. Earlier in his career, Lavey played oboe in the San Francisco Ballet Orchestra, worked as a lion-trainer, assisted in hypnotism shows, and became a police photographer. He began holding an occult-studies group, which included filmmaker Kenneth Anger, and in 1966 he shaved his head and proclaimed himself high priest of the Church of Satan. Lavey claimed an affiliated membership of nine thousand members in the United States, France, Italy, Germany, Britain, and South America, and was an advisor on several occult feature films, including, The Mephisto Waltz and Rosemary's Baby – where he appeared on screen as the Devil. Lavey's books include the Satanic Bible (1969) and the Satanic Rituals (1972).

LAZARIS: The entity (an evil spirit) that is channeled through California businessman Jack Purcel.

LEFT-HAND PATH: Occultists who spend their time being destructive, manipulative and "evil".

LEMEGETON: A particular grimoire that contains symbols of evil spirits.

LETHE: Stream of forgetfulness in Hell.

LETTERS OF PROTECTION: Magic letters, lucky letters and letters of protection, etc., in spite of their religious exterior belong to the domain of superstition and sorcery.

LEVITATION: The act of raising an object or a person from the ground and causing them to float in the air through supernatural power. People or objects are raised up and appear to float in the air or sail through the air, as if held or thrown by an invisible hand. In actuality evil spirits are raising or moving the person or object.

LIFESPRING: Motivational training technique, founded by Mind Dynamics graduate John Hanley, that declares, "We are intelligent and well-meaning beings…there is nothing that needs to be fixed."

LIFE TRAINING: An imitation of "est" started by two Episcopal priests, involving the rapid "processing" of painful past trauma.

LIGATURE: A spell which prevents a person from doing something.

LIGHT AS A FEATHER – STIFF AS A BOARD: A "game" usually played at slumber parties and sleepovers whereby one participant lays on the floor and is levitated by the other participants with their fingers under the individual on the floor. Actually an occult form of levitation.

LINKING: A mental identification with a person or spirit; usually as part of a practice of magic.

LITHOLATRY: Worship of stones.

LITHOMANCY: Divination using precious stones, possibly colored beads; usually stones are thrown on a flat surface, and whichever reflects the most light is considered the omen. Blue means good luck, green means realization of a hope, red means happiness in love or marriage, yellow means disaster or betrayal, purple means a period of sadness, and black or grey means misfortune.

LOA: Term used in Vodoun for spirit entities. The Loa are 'fed' by tending their altars, and worshiped by being allowed to possess the bodies of devotees in trance, whereupon they take on specific attributes.

LORD MAITREYA: The New Age Christ, who is said to be the fulfillment of all the great religious leaders of the world. Maitreya was originally a savior in Buddhist thought.

LUCID DREAMING: Dreaming while being aware that one is dreaming and therefore being able to control the dream. Instead of changing the dream one becomes able to control their behavior in the dream and therefore able to alter the dream so that one can do what they've ever wanted and go anywhere they want to go. Often involved with this occult practice are out of body experiences. See *Out-of-Body Experience (OBE)*.

LUCIFER: Means "Morning Star;" the archangel who was at the throne of God. Because of pride, he had a revolt against God, and was cast out of heaven along with one third of the angel population who he deceived into believing he was actually the Son of God, the Messiah. Also as the "light bearer," considered a neutral being or force which man can use for good or evil in his attempt to gain godhood.

LUCIFERIANS: A satanic sect active during the Medieval Period, this group sacrificed to evil forces and felt that Lucifer was the son of God and was wrongly expelled. Therefore they worshiped Satan. Still active.

LUCIS TRUST: Originally incorporated as the Lucifer Publishing Company, the Lucis Trust oversees the Lucis Publishing Company, World Goodwill, and Arcane School. Lucis Trust owns all the copyrights of the Alice Bailey books.

LYCANTHROPY: The assumption of an animal form by an occultist.

M

MACLAINE, SHIRLEY: Award winning actress whose personal problems led her to investigate psychic phenomena from channeling to astral projection, resulting in a series of best-selling books.

MACROBIOTICS: Metaphysical dietary system of eating and healing using whole grains, vegetables and fish, and avoiding meat and processed foods.

MACUMBA: A religion similar to Vodoun, Macumba was started by African slaves in an attempt to continue their ancestral tribal religion after being captured by the Portuguese. Now heavily over laden with Catholic symbolism. A low criminal form of spiritism (African), a mixture of black magic, designed to prosecute enemies, and protect from enemies.

MAFU: A discarnate being who speaks through medium Penny Torres.

MAGE: A general term for anyone doing magic, especially of the active kinds often used as a synonym for "magus".

MAGIC: The technique of harnessing the secret powers of nature and seeking to influence the events for one's own purposes.

MAGIC, BLACK: Magic performed with evil intent. The "Black Magician" or sorcerer calls upon the supernatural powers of darkness – devils, demons and veil spirits – and performs ceremonies invoking bestial or malevolent forces intended to harm another person.

MAGIC: BLACK, WHITE, NEUTRAL, HEALING - Divinely forbidden arts of bringing about results beyond human power (counterfeits of divine healing or miracles) by recourse to superhuman spirit agencies (Satan and demons).

MAGIC, CEREMONIAL: Magic that employs ritual, symbols and ceremony. Ceremonial magic stimulates the senses by including its ritual ceremonial costumes, dramatic invocations to the gods or spirits, potent incense, and mystic sacraments.

MAGIC, CIRCLE: Circle inscribed on the floor of a temple for magical ceremonial purposes. Believed to hold magical powers within and protect those involved in the ceremony from evil.

MAGIC DEATH OR DEATH MAGIC: Using a magic charm or spell or item to pass the sickness of the living over onto the dying.

MAGIC – THE GATHERING: See *Appendix F.*

MAGICAL HYPNOSIS: The occult form of hypnosis which can produce extremely harmful results.

MAGICK: Magic that employs ritual symbols and ceremony, including ceremonial costumes, dramatic invocations to the gods, potent incense and mystic statements. Denotes black magic usually.

MAGISTELLUS: An elemental servant or familiar.

MAGISTER: Male leader of a coven.

MAGNETICISM: An occult form of healing which supposedly uses magnetic forces. Also known as Mesmerism.

MAGUS: A male witch.

MAIDEN: Title sometimes conferred upon a Lady's daughter.

MAITREYA: The name has its roots in a legendary Buddha figure. Some New Age advocates believe that the "second coming of Christ" occurred in 1977 in the person of Maitreya.

MAITREYA, LORD: The supreme member of a spiritual hierarchy who has supposedly incarnated in the body of an Asian new age messiah and who claims that sharing is the only way to achieve peace on earth.

MANDRAKE: A Eurasian plant, Mandragora officinarum; thought to resemble the human body. The plant was once believed to have magical powers.

MANDALA: A design, usually concentric, that focuses attention to a single point.

MANTEUMAI: A Greek word that means divine, prophesy, or give an oracle.

MANTRA: A "holy" word, phrase, or verse in Hindu or Buddhist meditation techniques. A mantra is usually provided to an initiate by a guru who is supposed to hold specific insights regarding the needs of his pupils. The vibrations of the mantra are said to lead the mediator into union with the divine source within.

MARE: An evil spirit which sits on the chest and causes a feeling of suffocation.

MARGARITOMANCY: Divination using pearls which were supposed to bounce upward beneath an inverted pot if a guilty person approached.

MASKIN: Seven subterranean evil spirits.

MASKITH: An image usually painted or carved.

MASLOW, ABRAHAM: Founder of the Association of Humanistic Psychology, he also coined the New Age terms "peak-experience", "synergy" (mutual cooperation), "self actualization", and "humanistic psychology"; is considered the founding father of the Human Potential Movement.

MASONS: *See Appendix A*

MASS: Ceremony. See **BLACK MASS**

MASSEKAH: A statue or image made from a mold.

MASTER: Top leader.

MASTERS OF WISDOM: The arch evil spirits of Satan. In the Bible they are **Master Meon** (Numbers 32:38), **Master Peor** (Numbers 25:3, Deuteronomy 4:3), **Master Perzim** (II Samuel 5:20), **Master Shalisha** (II Kings 4:42), **Master Tamar** (Judges 20:33), **Master Zebub** (II Kings 1:2) and **Master Zephon** (Exodus 14:2).

MATERIALIZATION: Physical manifestation of a spirit being.

MASTEBAH: Something that sits upright, like a statue or pillar.

MAYA: A Hindu teaching that the only reality is the deity Brahman, the Supreme Absolute, and that all else in the material world is an extension of Brahman's thoughts and therefore illusory or transitory.

MAY EVE: Festival Roodman.

MEDITATION: The mystical process of stilling the mind and senses so that sensory stimulation is limited and awareness of internal essence becomes acute. An altered state of consciousness obtained via breathing techniques, chanting words or phrases (mantra), or use of Yoga or other Eastern Religious techniques.

MEDIUMS: In spiritualism, one who acts as an intermediary between the world of spirits and discarnate entities and the everyday world or normal reality. Spirits are summoned during a séance and their influence may be perceived through materializations, through Ouija board communications, through an agreed code of rappings and knocks, or through automatic writing or automatic painting and drawing. If an evil entity takes over the body of the medium during a séance, that being is known as the control. A psychic person whose body is used as a vehicle for communicating with spirits.

MENDES, GOAT OF: Form in which the devil is said to manifest during the witches' Sabbath.

MENTALISM: An ancient performing art in which the practitioner uses mental acuity, principles of stage magic/or suggestion to present the illusion of mind reading, psychokinesis, precognition, and clairvoyance or mind control. These are the techniques of fortunetellers, mind readers, sorcery, wizardry, and witchcraft. The Bible strongly warns people not to consult practitioners of mentalism for the truth, but to inqauire of God (ISa. 8:19). Those who practice these arts receive their power from demons and are being deceived. The Bible condemns and forbids these practices several times (Deut. 18:9-14; Isaiah 44:25; Jeremiah 27:9; 2 Kings 21:6, 23:24). King Saul died because "he consulted a medium for guidance" rather than God (1 Chr. 10:13-14.)[5i]

MENTAL TELEPATHY: The use of mental images to receive and transmit messages.

MENTOR: Senior brother and sister.

MERIDIAN: In acupuncture, a presumed pathway in the body similar to the circulatory system, through which the universal life-energy flows.

MERODACH: Regarded for a time as a supreme deity of the Babylonians; sometimes associated with Bel (Bel-Marduk). (Marduk is in the Dungeons & Dragons Manuals.)

MESMER, ANTON: Nineteenth-century German physician who experimented with mind control techniques resembling hypnotism, first known as "Mesmerism". Magnetism was introduced by Mesmer.

MESMERISM: Similar to hypnotism, used largely by occultists. Similar to the "gifts of spirit" for Christians, it is "a gift of Satan to occultists". Magnetism was introduced by Mesmer.

METAGNOMY: Divination by viewing events while in a hypnotic state.

---

[5] Scott, Bryan, booklet Criss Angel "MindFreak", Titusville, FL, Center for Christian Counseling, 2006.

METAPHYSICS: System of principles relating to the transcendent or supernatural. The science relating to the transcendent, to the mysteries of occult knowledge, and to speculation about the psychic, strange, and unknown.

METAPSYCHOLOGY: Quarterly New Age journal emphasizing trance-channeled information.

METEMPSYCHOSIS: Ancient Greek word which essentially means the same thing as reincarnation.

METEOROMANCY: Observing meteors or similar phenomena for omens.

METOPOSCOPY: The reading of character from the lines on a person's forehead.

MIDSUMMER: Festival of Beltane (May 1st).

MIGHTY ONES: Ancient gods revered by witches.

MIND SCIENCE: A religious philosophy based on the ideas of Ernest Holmes, who denied orthodox Christian doctrines in favor of promoting the possibility of "Christ-realization" by all men.

MINOR LUMINARY: Lieutenants to leaders.

MIRRORMANTIC: Division through the use of such objects as crystal balls, mirrors, rock crystals, or bodies of still water.

MISSAL: Book with rituals and teachings.

MOJO: Magickal power from the lower chakras, especially equated with Love and Power in Voodoo spells.

MOKSHA: The final state of "deliverance" from the burdensome cycle of reincarnation.

MOLYBDOMANCY: Divination by observing the hissing of molten lead.

MONISM: Literally means "one". In a spiritual framework it refers to the classical occult philosophy that "All Is One"; all reality may be reduced to a single, unifying principle partaking of the same essence and reality. Monism also relates to the belief in Pantheism that there is no ultimate distinction between the Creator and the creation.

MOON MANCY: The observance of the full moon when planting, casting spells, getting married, and so on.

MULTIPLE TRANSMUTATION OF ALTER PERSONALITIES: An occult practice of removing alter personalities formed during extreme ritual abuse from an individual's soul and placing them into the broken soul of another individual with hopes that neither soul will ever find healing.

MUMMIFICATION: The ancient Egyptian means of preserving the physical body after death to facilitate its journey into the next life.

MYOMANCY: Drawing prophetic conclusions from rats and mice, particularly their cries or destruction they cause.

MYSTICISM: Belief that God is totally different than anything the human mind can think and must be approached by a mind without content. Spiritual union or direct communion with Ultimate Reality can be obtained through subjective experience such as intuition or a unifying vision. Mysticism denies the utterly transcendent reality of God.

MYTH: Metaphor, particularly one with a ploy and a cast of characters.

MYTHOLOGY: A gestalt composed of myth and theology that forms the religious world-view of people.

N

NATAL ANNIVERSARY: The idea that the positions of the planets and other heavenly bodies, as they were located at one's birth affect that individual on recurring birthdates.

NATURALISM: View that asserts that nothing beyond nature is real. Human beings are therefore to be understood strictly in terms of heredity and environment.

NATUROPATHY: Non-intrusive form of medical care using herbs instead of drugs, generally practiced by chiropractors and osteopaths.

NECROLATRY: Worship of the dead.

NECROMANCY: A practice in which the "spirits of the dead" are summoned to provide omens relating to future events or to discover secrets of the past.

NECRONOMICON: Communication with the supposed spirits of the dead, usually with the use of bones or some part of the corpse.

NECROPHILIA: Sexual intercourse with the dead. This sometimes arises with psychopathic murderers who believe their victims to still be alive. Necrophilia seems to be a feature of the more debased forms of black magic.

NEO-AMERICAN CHURCH: Their symbol appears to be a three-eyed frog. The Neo-American church recruits children into their activities and also hinders the finding of missing children. The Neo-American church people usually drive vans with gun racks located behind the driver's seat. They will show up with Rainbow tribe and also associate themselves with other groups.

NEOPAGAN: Follower of some Western religious tradition other than Judaism or Christianity. Neo-pagan groups have a close affinity for nature, occult and initiatory traditions, and may be patrons of ancient Greek or Egyptian religions, Druidism, witchcraft, ceremonial magic or even Satanism.

NEOPHYTE: One who is about to go through the initiation into a coven.

NETWORK: An informal, decentralized organization created by like-minded individuals who are interested in addressing specific problems and offering possible solutions. All of this takes place outside of conventional institutions.

NETWORKING: The New Age concept of linkage of ideas, practices, and metaphysical efforts; combines the endeavors of various aspects of the movement worldwide through written and verbal communication, as well as telepathic communiqués.

NEUROLINGUISTICS: A behavioristic form of motivational training and therapy, it supposes that observing body languages enables a counselor to help a client overcome his phobias, learning disabilities, and insecurities.

NEW AGE JOURNAL: Bimonthly New Age magazine emphasizing human potential aspects of the movement.

NEW AGE MOVEMENT: A spiritual, political and social phenomenon networking many occult/metaphysical organizations and groups intending to transform individuals by means of "mystical enlightenment" so that a new age of unprecedented peace, prosperity and harmony can be introduced on earth.

NEW AGE MUSIC: A contemporary music genre, usually instrumental and often acoustic, based on classical and jazz styles; generally played in a free-form or unstructured style for the purpose of altering the listener's consciousness and perception of reality.

NEW THOUGHT: A late 1800's philosophy of mental healing promoted by Warren Felt Evans, who influenced May Baker Eddy, the founder of Christian Science, and Charles and Myrtle Fillmore, who founded Unity.

NIRVANA: Literally, a "blowing out" or a "cooling" of the fires of existence; the main word used in Buddhism for final release from the cycle of birth and death into bliss.

NOSTRODAMUS: Sixteenth-century occult mystic who wrote ten volumes of prophecy called "Centuries", supposedly predicting the world's future in minute detail; his own description of "receiving" these so-called prophecies is clearly divination; lived 1503-1555.

NOVEMBER EVE: This is All Hallow's Eve, also called Sambain, which is Scottish Gaelic meaning All Hallow's Eve, occuring on Oct. 31.

NUDITY: Believed essential to raising forces through which magic works.

NUMBERS OF SIGNIFICANCE –

> ONE - equate with primal chaos
>
> THREE - triple repetitions, effective in incantations
>
> FIVE - symbolizes justice
>
> SEVEN - in occult rites, possesses mystic implications
>
> THIRTEEN - number of members in a coven, members being associated with thirteen lunar moons
>
> 4 x 4 - in Talmudic computations the Devil's own
>
> > number
>
> 7 + 9 - multiples of these possessed thaomaturgic
>
> > potency; odd numbers lucky; triple repetitions is characteristic of magical rituals
>
> 666 - sign of the beast, Devil's calling numbers

O

OBJECT LINK: An object that is supposedly impregnated with the magnetism of a proposed victim or subject or a spell.

OCCULT: A term, which means hidden, secret or mysterious.

OCCULTISM: Belief in secret supernatural forces and beings.

OCULOMANCY: Divination by observing a person's eyes.

OFFICER: Third leader in a coven, after Magister and Lady.

OLINOMANCY: Looking for omens form wines.

OMEN: A prophetic sign.

ONEIROMANCY: Interpretation of dreams.

ONE WORLDERS: Those who advocate the abolition of nations, working to hand over power to a single-world government; off shoots of the United World Federalists found in the 1930s.

ONOMANCY: Finds meaning and omens in the names of persons and things; onomancy is seldom used today, except for interpreting a person's proper name.

ONOMANTICS: Onomancy applied to personal names.

ONYOMANCY: Interpretation of various characteristics from a person's fingernails as one aspect of Palmistry.

OOMANTIA (OOSCOPY): Ancient practice of divination by eggs.

OPIOMANCY: Divination from serpents.

O.P. MESSENGER: Student ministers.

ORANGE MAGIC: Used for pride and courage. Heroism and attraction.

ORDO TEMPLI ORIENTIS (O.T.O.): Initials for Ordo Templi Orientis, a sect whose members practiced sexual magic. The order was founded by Karl Kellner. The famous Aleister Crowley was a member who helped to revive O.T.O. in the middle 1920s.

ORIENS: Rules over all the spirits of the east.

ORISHAS: Yoruban term used in Santeria for African nature spirits of deities called "Loa" in Vodoun and Voodoo.

ORNISCOPY (ORNITHAMANCY): Observation of the flight of birds for omens.

OSIRIS: Egyptian "green man", God of Vegetation who dies and rules in the underworld as Lord of the Dead. Husband to Isis and father of Horus, his reincarnation.

OUIJA BOARD: Board with letters and numbers with which spirits can communicate.

OUT-OF-BODY EXPERIENCE (OBE): Leaving the physical body while conscious, at rest, asleep, or near death. Departing one's physical body and observing both one's self and the world from outside of one's body. The experience is quite common. Some people experience OBE while under the influence of an anesthetic or while semi-conscious due to trauma. Some have an OBE while under the influence of drugs. Surveys show that about 15% to 20% of the population have had an OBE at some time during their life. This occult activity has reported been used by spy agencies so that an individual can leave the body and sit in on secret meetings, etc.

OVER SHADOW: The term used when an invisible entity takes over the mind, emotions, will, or the body of a spirit medium.

OVOMANCY: A type of divination from eggs.

OWL: In many cultures the bird is associated with death and evil powers.

P

PACT: A vow of secrecy given by a witch who joins a coven.

PACT WITH SATAN: Selling one's soul to the devil; promising to serve him.

PAGAN: The term is used derogatorily to describe a heathen or "unbeliever", but has now assumed a new currency among practitioners of witchcraft and magic. The so-called New Pagans are dedicated to reviving the old religion and reestablishing the worship of Nature and the lunar goddess.

PAGANISM: A practicing pagan.

PALMISTRY: A form of divination which attempts to analyze an individual's character, or predict his future, by studying the lines and other features of his hands. The size, shape, and proportions of the hands and fingers, the length of the lines and their characteristics, and the areas called "mounts" all influence the reader's interpretation. The palmist gives particular attention to 4 lines and 7 mounts in the hand, and makes use of astrology, believing that the planetary influences upon a person's life are also written in the palms. Each of the mounts is named for a heavenly body (e.g., Jupiter, Mars, Venus, etc.), while the nature of such mount is supposed to reveal character traits (e.g., ambition, pride, meekness, sexuality, etc.). The four principle lines in the hand are said to represent the head, life, heart, and fortune. The head line is supposed to indicate intelligence, the heart line reveals affection, the fortune line indicates success or failure in life, and the life line forecasts a person's physical well-being and length of life.

As the practice is under the influence and control of the powers of darkness it is not surprising that those who have become involved in palmistry, or who have had their palms read, generally suffer some form of occult oppression as a result.

PALO MAYOMBE: A Cuban sect of Santeria followed by many Latin American drug gangs; sort of a "magickal mafia", leaders engage in human sacrifice and other terror tactics to keep followers in line and enemies at bay.

PAN: "In ancient Greek mythology, the son of Hermes and Dryope. Pan was the god of flocks and shepherds, but also had a more far-reaching role as lord of nature and all forms of wildlife. He was depicted as half-man, half-goat, and played a pipe with seven reeds. Regarded as high god."

PANTHEISM: Belief that God and the world are ultimately identical; "All is God". Everything that exists constitutes a unity, and this all-inclusive unity is divine. God is the force and law of the universe but not a Being with personality.

PANTHEON: A temple dedicated to all the gods.

PARANORMAL: Faculties and phenomena in psychical research that are beyond the "normal" in terms of cause and effect as presently understood.

PARAPSYCHOLOGY: The study of occult phenomena such as telepathy, clairvoyance, precognition and psychokinesis.

PAST LIFE THERAPY: Therapy that assumes the reality of reincarnation and which involves being "taken back" into past lives by a channeler or spirit guide, to discover the supposed roots of present trauma or trouble, such information should be considered to have been given by demons.

PEACE SYMBOL: The early 60's peace symbol is now commonly thought of as the "Cross of Nero" by heavy metal heads and occultists.

PEALE, NORMAN VINCENT: Pastor and author who pioneered the positive thinking concept and from whose premises certain New Agers have drawn inspiration.

PEGAMANCY: Divination by observing spring water bubbling fountains.

PENDUMLUM: Heavy object on a string, used for dawning or fortune telling.

PENTACLE (PENTAGRAM): A five-pointed star used as a magic symbol in rituals, also knows as the Pentagram.

PENTAGRAM: A pentacle surrounded by a circle. It represents the four elements. When the star is inverted with two points up, it stands for black arts. When turned with a single point up, it symbolizes white magic. Pentagrams are also worn for "protection" and identification among the craft.

PERCIPIENT: Person who receives telepathic messages.

PERENNIAL PHILOSOPHY: A term coined by Aldous Huxley that sees all religious truth or experience as one and the same. This philosophy proposes that even though the externals of the various religions may differ, the essence or core truth is the same in each.

PESSOMANCY: Divination by pebbles.

PHILOSOPHER'S STONE: A psychic substance used in Alchemy.

PHRENOLOGY: Divination from interpreting head formations or bumps on the head.

PHYLLORHODOMANCY: A means of divination that comes from Ancient Greece; a person slaps rose petals against his hand, and the success of a venture is judged by the loudness of the sound.

PHYSIOGNAMY: Analysis of a person's character through observation of a person's features or physical characteristics.

THE PLAN: A New Age reference to a "conspiracy" that would replace present religious, political, and economic systems with an intuitive thrust for planetary harmony under New Age concepts.

PLANETARY CITIZENS: A New Age activist group committed to engendering a "planetary consciousness" among both New Agers and the general Public.

PLANETIZATION: New Age advocates believe that the various threats facing the human race require a global solution. This solution is "planetization". The word refers to the unifying of the world into a corporate brotherhood.

POLARITY THERAPY: Bionergetic healing therapy teaching that illness results from blockage of energy at certain places in the body, a hindrance that can supposedly be removed by strategic laying-on of hands.

POLTERGEIST: "Rattling Ghost", a ghost that tends to throw or break objects or generally cause mischief.

POLYTHEISM: The belief that there are many deities.

POSITIVE IMAGING: A form of psychological reinforcement that seeks to replace negative mental images with carefully constructed positive ones, out of which a new reality can be created; basically mind over matter.

POWER OBJECT: An object with "witch power" placed in a subject or victim's vicinity to complete a spell.

PRANA: The power whereby everything in the universe supposedly exists, known as chi in Taoism and vital breath in Hinduism; the force of life, which is said to emanate from the impersonal energy of Brahman (god).

PRECOGNITION: The supernatural ability to have knowledge of, or to see, events which are yet in the future and predict their occurrence, such as Jeane Dixon's predictions of President Kennedy's assassination as well as that of Gandhi, Eisenhower's election, and Russia's launching of the first satellite. Although many have been deluded into believing that this is a manifestation of the Biblical gift of prophecy, a careful examination of the origin of this woman's psychic powers indicate that their source is not from heaven.

PREDICTIVE DREAMS/VISIONS: Dreams or visions which reveal the future or hidden knowledge (counterfeit biblical prophesy).

PREMONITION: A foreboding of the future.

PROGNOSTICATION: To foretell from signs or symptoms; prophesying without the Holy Spirit; soothsaying. Is. 47:12-15; Josh. 13:22.

PROPHECIES: Ability to foretell the future.

PROPHETS: Senior brothers and sisters.

PROVISIONAL MASTER: Lieutenants leaders.

PSI: The twenty-third letter of the Greek alphabet; a general New Age term for ESP, psychokinesis, telepathy, clairvoyance, precognition, and other paranormal phenomena that are non-physical in nature.

PSYCHIC: Pertaining to phenomena which are supernatural, or perhaps actually demonic; or a person who has this power.

PSYCHIC BIRTH: A quickening of spiritual or cosmic consciousness and power. This new consciousness is one that recognized oneness with God and the universe. Psychic birth is an occult counterpart to the Christian new birth.

PSYCHIC ENERGY: Extrasensory energy that enables people to do miracles.

PSYCHIC HEALER: A person who cures mental or physical illness from the cosmic energy emanating through the healer's hands.

PSYCHIC SURGERY: Surgery by a medium having no ordinary medical knowledge, while in a trance.

PSYCHOANALYSIS: Tracing mental and physical ills back to hurtful childhood experiences; based on Sigmund Freud's theories.

PSYCHOGRAPHY: A form of mysterious writing, usually of a divinatory type.

PSYCHOKINESIS: Power of the mind to influence matter or move objects. Popularly known as PK (see also Telekinesis).

PSYCHOMETRY: The gaining of impressions from a physical object, usually having to do with the owner or the object's history.

PSYCHOTECHNOLOGIES: Refers to the various approaches or systems aimed at deliberately altering ones consciousness.

PUNK ROCK: Punk rock began in England as a revolt against the economic, educational and political system. Shabby clothes, spiked hair, Mohawk haircuts, shaved heads, and outlandish make-up represented the British youth rebellion against the status-quo. When punk rock came to America the issues faded, but the anti-establishment statement was the same. Whatever society cherishes - religion, law, tradition punkers denigrate. Punkers want to do anything they want, to be angry and alienated. Kids who follow punk rock groups view themselves as society's victims. Punkers' ultimate goal is to live recklessly and to be young and fast. The punk rock dance, called the slam dance, involves slamming into someone else, kicking them and punching them. Many seem bent on self-destruction, and it's not unusual for them to wound themselves with razor blades, knives, cigarettes or cigarette lighters. (Quotes by Darlyne Pettinicchio, probation officer from Orange County, Calif. Director of the Back in Control Center, news article, The Press Enterprise Riverside, Calif., Ma, 1986). Note: While punk is not typically occult, one should remember that adolescents involved in this type of negative, violent activity sometimes become involved with occult groups.

PURPLE MAGIC: Used for wealth and good fortune. Prosperity, domination and command.

PYRAMID POWER: The belief that pyramid shapes are antennae that pick up frequencies of universal energy that bring healing, sound sleep, nutrition, and superior sexual experience.

PYROLATRY: Worship of fire.

PYROMANCY: Divination by fire, usually involving powered substances thrown in.

R

RAMTHA: The entity (demon) channeled through J.Z. Knight and who is followed closely by actress Linda Evans.

READINGS: Information or revelations gotten during a séance.

REBIRTH: In the occult, technically from reincarnation in that the individual who does it is not reborn as the same self.

RED MAGIC: Used for physical work, as in healing of people and animals. Passion and sex.

REFLEXOLOGY: A belief that the sole of the foot contains reflex points that correspond to all internal organs and bodily functions, and that manipulation of these points relieves pain and disease.

REIKI: An occult form of healing. *See Appendix D.*

REINCARNATION: The belief that the soul after death passes on to another body. Any belief that after death your soul will experience rebirth into a new body (human or animal).

REMOTE INFLUENCE: The practice (sometimes by Christians who should know better) is the attempt to influence the subconscious minds of others while they are asleep or in another room and is an unwarranted telepathic invasion of the God-given privacy of the subconscious mind of another individual.

The psychic dangers or adverse effects in such an unscriptural practice are the same as in other forms of telepathy. Such intrusion is a trespass upon the prerogatives of God. The excuse that such remote suggestions are intended to influence someone for "good" overlooks the occult nature of the practice.

REMOTE VIEWING/HEALING: Discerning telepathically or transmitting healing across distances without the psychic's being in direct physical contact with person, object, or circumstance.

REPERCUSSION: Injuries received by a projected form that appear on someone's physical body.

RESPONDER: At rituals he states the natures of Lucifer and Christ.

RETROCGNITION: The process of knowing past information which is usually attained through some paranormal methods.

RHABDOMANCY: Divination by means of a rod or stick; the forerunner of the divining rod.

RHAPSODOMANCY: Opening a book, usually poetry, and reading words or passages at random, looking for omens.

RIGHT BRAIN LEARNING: The right hemisphere of the brain is believed to be the center of intuitive and creative thought (as opposed to the rational nature of the left hemisphere). New Ager's have seized on this as a justification to bring "right brain leaning techniques" into the classroom. These techniques include meditation, yoga, and guided imagery.

RIGHT HAND PATH: In mystical and occultism, the esoteric path associated with spiritual illumination and positive aspiration. It is the path of light as distinct from the so-called left-hand path of darkness which equates with evil, bestiality, and black magic. Occultists who spend their time being constructive, manipulative and "good".

RITES OF PASSAGE: Ritual commemoration of life's transitions. Such passages include: being born- becoming an incarnate being; onset of puberty- becoming sexually fertile; marriage- becoming bonded to a partner; giving birth- becoming a mother or father; menopause- becoming a wise crone; death- going to the underworld to await rebirth.

RITUAL: A magical ceremony used in both white and black magic.

RITUAL ABUSE: Victimizing someone (usually sexually) in a satanic ritual. For those who do not believe Satanism is prevalent in the United States, a reading of the *Illinois State Law #87-1167 Ritualized Abuse of a Child* (Appendix C) will change that opinion. Please remember this law was not written in the Salem witch hunt days but in 1993.

ROBERTS, JANE: Best selling author and channel for the spirit Seth (a demon); there are numerous "Seth" books.

ROCK MUSIC – The Six themes of Rock Music are: love-sex; drugs & alcohol; racism & bigotry; graphic violence & death; rebellion and/or aggression; fascination with the occult.

ROLFING: A deep, forceful massage technique that is said to restructure the body so it more properly aligns with gravity and the energies of earth.

ROSE CROSS – A golden cross with a rose at its center, the emblem of the esoteric order of the Rosicrucians.

ROSICRUCIANS - A brotherhood order (headquartered in California) teaching a system of metaphysical and scientific philosophy aimed at awakening the latent powers of man.

RUNES: From the German "raunen" meaning a secret or mystery; occult symbols that are known in many areas of Northern Europe. (Note: Runes are used for Magick. We are seeing them in the United States in certain incidents which involve ritualistic crime). Stones inscribed with letters of the ancient Scandinavian alphabet, believed to have been used by the Vikings for predictive purposes and revived today for fortune telling.

RYERSON, KEVIN: Channeler consulted by actress Shirley MacLaine.

S

SABBAT: One of the eight annual festivals of the seasonal round celebrated by nearly all Pagans, including Witches. The solstices and equinoxes are known as Quarters, and the others are Cross-Quarters, also known as Grand Sabbats by Witches. Several are also celebrated by both Christians and Satanist: Ostara spring Equinox, Mar 21 (Easter), Beltane- May1 (May Day), Litha- summer solstice, June 21 (St. John's), Lughnasad- August 2 (Lammas), Mabon-autumn equinox, Sept. 21 (Harvest), Samhain- Nov 1 (All Saint's Day), Yule- winter solstice, Dec. 21 (Christmas), Oimeic- Feb 2 (Imboic, Brigit, Candlemas).

SACRAL: Pertaining to sacred rites or observances.

SACRAMENTAL: Consecrated.

SACRAMENTARIAN: A person who regards the sacraments as merely visible symbols.

SACRIFICE: An offering made to a deity, often upon an altar. Scarifies are performed ritually to placate a god and to offer blood, which is symbolic of the life-force and invariably associated with fertility. Some magicians believed that the ritual slaughter of a sacrificial animal releases life energy, which can be tapped magically and used to attune the magician to the god invoked in ritual.

SACRIFIST: Presiding priest.

SACRILEGE: Misuse, theft, desecration or profanation of anything consecrated.

SACROSANCT: Sacred and inviolable.

SADISTIC: One who will deliberately torture or hurt any living creature.

SALAMANDER: An elemental who lives in fire.

SAMANDHI (SATORI): Ultimate or highest state of God-consciousness or enlightenment in classical Hindu yoga. Satori is the equivalent in Zen Buddhism: a state of existential intuitive enlightenment.

SAMHAIN: (pronounced "so-ahn") The Great Sabbat, or cross-quarter festival, occurring midway between autumn Equinox and Winter Solstice. Traditionally celebrated on Nov. 1.

SAMSARA: The continual cycle of rebirth.

SANAT KIMARA: To the initiated of the occult, this is the king of the world, this is Lucifer who is the "light" of the world.

SANCTUM: Main ritual room.

SANTERIA: a mingling of African tribal religions and Catholicism established by African slaves brought to the Americas and Caribbean.

SATAN: The angelic being created by God. He was an archangel who rebelled and was cast out of heaven.

SATANIC: Refers to anything that pertains to Satan, which is evil.

SATANIC BIBLE: A diabolically inspired work written by Anton LeVey.   It consists of three parts: Book of Lucifer, Book of Belial, and Book of Leviathan. Chapter titles include such demonic and perverted subjects as: Satanic Sex; An invocation for the Conjuration of Lust; The Black Mass; The Practice of Satanic Magic; Satanic Ritual; Invocation to Satan; Invocation for the Conjuration of Destruction, and How to Sell Your Soul. The book advocates indulging in the seven deadly sins forbidden by Scriptures (pride, envy, greed, anger, gluttony, sloth, and lust), as they will give physical, emotional, and mental gratification, and will release one from prudish guilt-feelings about sin.

The Satanic Bible teaches there is no God but that man himself is god and his own redeemer. Christ is blasphemed as weak and impotent, and the king of slaves and weaklings. There is no heaven or hell; therefore, man should make the most of life here and now by indulging in sensuous pleasures instead of practicing abstinence or temperance. The Satanist is encouraged to indulge in all his natural appetites and desires in order to eliminate his frustrations. The righteous and good die young because the denial of natural appetites leads to deterioration of the mind and body.

SATANIC RITUAL CALENDAR: See *Satanic Ritual Calendar Appendix G*

SATANIC WORSHIP: Worshipping Satan, attending a satanic church, being part of a coven.

SATANIC MASS: In Satanism, a blasphemous ritual that parodies the Catholic Mass, invokes the powers of darkness and sometimes employs the use of a naked woman as an altar.

SATANISM: The worship of Satan. It claims to be a religion of the flesh, world, and the carnal – all ruled over by Satan. Satanism advocates, for example, sexual freedom, interpreting this to mean indulging one's sexual lusts in any way desired (homosexual, heterosexual, self-gratification, bi-sexual, the practice of sadism, masochism, or any other lewd perversion), and with as many others as desired, as long as the parties consent.

SATANIC RITUAL CALENDAR – A yearly calendar used in Satanism. See page 96 for the calendar itself.

SATANIC WORSHIP/SATANIC BIBLE - Worshipping Satan, attending a Satanic Church, being part of a coven, or reading Anton LeVey's Satanic Bible.

SCARFING: See Auto Erotic Stimulation.

SCIENTOLOGY: A healing movement founded by Dr. Ronald Hubbard and discussed in his book Dianetics which employs an E-meter in the healing process.

SCIOMANCY: Various forms of divination involving direct communication with spirits.

SCREENING (raddiesthesia): A small box used to screen out harmful "earth" rays; a mediumistic field which can be clairvoyantly perceived through the mediumistic powers of dowsers and pendulum practitioners and the like.

SCRYING: Divination by gazing, as in crystal, mirror, water, etc.

SEAL: A demon's summoning diagram or signature.

SEAL OF SOLOMON: Two interlocking triangles that form a hexagram. This seal is said to offer the greatest protection for the practioner.

SEANCE or SPIRITUALISM - Any gathering of people where an attempt is made to contact a dead person or a spirit to receive communication from the spirit world. See Spiritism.

SECOND COMING OF CHRIST: Understood by some as the coming of the Cosmic Christ in all humanity, related to the New Age concept of the "Mass incarnation". The Second Coming is supposedly now occurring in the hearts and minds of people all over the earth. Others associate it specifically with the appearance of Maitreya as the avatar of this age.

SEEING: The ability to hold the item of another and see events or know facts about that person.

SEER: One who can see the hidden; a diviner.

SELF ACTUALIZATION: The state of fulfilling one's potential so fully that one realizes one's self-deity.

SELF-HYPNOSIS: For relaxation, consciousness expansion, incarnation regression, and a variety of other New Age intents, some consider self-hypnosis the best tool for entering altered states of the mind. Movement catalogues offer subliminal devices to induce self-hypnosis, including audio cassettes that coach the subject into alpha states. For some, self-hypnosis is the pathway to rapidly releasing latent psychic powers. Practitioners are told to accept intuitively whatever images enter their minds under hypnosis. They are also warned to expect rebirthing stages and the possible intervention of entities seeking to use them as channels.

SELF IDOLATRY: Worship of self.

SELF REALIZATION: The act of acknowledging that one's self (ego) is identifiable with God and that one's highest inner nature is though to be pure and devoid of all evil.

SEMEL: A likeness or image.

SENSITIVE: A person who frequently demonstrates extrasensory gifts such as clairvoyance, telepathy, or precognition.

SENSITIVITY TRAINING: A problem solving technique which involves discussing a person's life, job, and marriage in a group setting, as well as touching one another's bodies when the lights have been turned off.

SEPHIROTH: The occult satanic tree of life: one side negative, one positive, one side masculine, one feminine, one side severe, one merciful; the tree as ten steps one must pass through in order to achieve priesthood in satanic religion.

SERPENT: Serpent w/horns is symbolic of the demons.

SERVERS: Ritual assistants.

SERVITOR: A familiar.

SET: Egyptian name for Satan, in 1975 Michael Aquino established the temple of set church religion in the United States.

SETH: Spirit entity channeled by Jane Roberts, with numerous books printed on his "messages".

SEXUAL HANGING: See autoerotic asphyxiation.

SHADE: The supposed spirit of a dead person.

SHADOWS, BOOK OF: The personal book used and kept by the high priest within the coven or group. All of his rituals and spells are kept in this book. When the high priest dies, the book is destroyed. The book is also used by pagans and by dabbler Satanists as a diary of personal activities.

SHAMBALLA: Legendary kingdom of spiritually developed adepts (similar to the occult concept of Atlantis), proposed by locale and an aspect of astral existence.

SHAKTI: The Female Principle in Hinduism.

SHAMAN: A medicine man or witch doctor.

SHAMAYIM: A Hebrew phrase that means "viewers of the heavens".

SHAMBALLAH: A palace where Lucifer and the masters are believed to reside. Initiated occultist believe Shamballah to be lost in the Gobi dessert or a hidden valley in Tibet.

SHARE INTERNATIONAL: Publication of Tara Center, expounding the teachings of Lord Maitreya and various New Age doctrines.

SHEBISIM: A "sun-pendant".

SHIGGUTS: An abomination or a detestable thing.

SHRINE: Ritual table.

SIDEROMANCY: Divining by observing the forms made by burning straws with a hot iron.

SIGIL: A "symbolic signature" inscribed on a talisman.

SIGIL OF BAPHOMET: A symbol of the Church of Satan-two concentric circles with a pentagram within the smaller one. Within the five-pointed star there is a picture of the Goat of Mendes.

SIGNS: The signs of the Zodiac. Everyone is born under one of these 12 signs or constellations: **Aquarius** Jan. 20 - Feb. 18; **Pisces** Feb. 19 - Mar. 20; **Aries** Mar. 21 – Apr. 19; **Taurus** Apr. 20 – May 20; **Gemini** May 21- June 20; **Cancer** June 21 – July 22; **Leo** July 23 – Aug. 22; **Virgo** Aug. 23 – Sept. 22; **Libra** Sept. 23 – Oct. 22; **Scorpio** Oct. 23 – Nov. 21; **Sagittarius** Nov. 22 – Dec. 21; **Capricorn** Dec. 22 – Jan. 19.

SILVA MIND CONTROL: "Mind expansion" techniques developed by Jose Silva to control one's future and fortune through self-hypnosis and the alteration of reality by mental supposition.

SILVER: The perfect metal to be used in occult objects and jewelry.

SKULL: Human or animal used in rites.

SKYCLAD: Nude.

SOCIETY FOR PSYCHICAL RESEARCH: Organization developed to para-psychological research and the scholarly collection of related information concerning the paranormal.

SOLAR LOGOS: Believed by some to be a mighty spiritual being who is the ensouling life of the solar system. The material solar system is simply a physical manifestation (or body) of this living intelligence.

SOLOMON: The king of Israel who is said, by some involved in the occult, to have written several grimoires, one such called "The Lesser Keys of Solomon". Practitioners also use the Seals of Solomon.

SOLSTICE: Either of two times of the year when the sun has no apparent northward or southward motion. Summer solstice is approximately June 22 and Winter Solstice is approximately December 22.

SO MOTE IT BE: Words said at the end of an occult ceremony and in Freemasonry to end a prayer. Similar to "amen" in traditional religious services.

SOOTHSAYER: A medium.

SOOTH SAYING: The act of foretelling events; prophesying by a spirit other than the Holy Spirit. Joshua 13:22; Micah 5:12-15; Acts 16:16-18.

SORCERER: A wizard, witch or magician; a practitioner of black magic.

SORCERY: Magic, usually of the black variety.

SORILEGE: Casting lots hoping to find a good omen.

SOUL FORCE - Any attempt by faithful church members to bring backsliders back to the church by means of mental powers at a distance (remote mental suggestion).

SOUL TIE - A spiritual union created by placing yourself in subjection to another person's authority or through sexual intercourse.

SOUL TRANSFER: Based on the premise that some soul types incarnate through a process of soul transfer. Commonly called 'Walk-ins', 'Crawl-ins', or 'Wanderers'. These are souls that agree to transfer into another soul's physical vehicle or body at a given point in the subject's life. The Apostle Paul had something to say about soul travel: *"We are confident, I say, and would prefer to be away from the body and at home with the Lord."* (2 Cor. 5:8). The Bible is clear on the subject. When your soul leaves the body it is destined for one of two places depending upon your salvation, Heaven or Hell. It is clear that the Christian is not to practice in soul travel.[6]

SPELL: An incantation designed to bring about magic.

SPIRAL DANCE: A Wiccan greeting dance celebrating spiral symbolism. Also a book by Starhawk.

SPIRIT GUIDE: A spiritual entity who provides information or "guidance", often through a medium or channeler. The spirit provides guidance only after the channeler relinquishes his perceptual and cognitive capacities into its control.

SPIRIT PHOTOGRAPHY: A photograph taken during a séance which, when developed reveals the face of the dead.

SPIRIT SPEAKS: Bimonthly New Age publication featuring occult phenomena.

SPIRITISM / SPIRITUALISM: A spiritual activity grounded in the persuasion that people can by means of certain Spiritistic Mediums make contact with the deceased (where contact actually occurs with demon spirits and not deported impersonations) and so acquire revelations from the beyond.)

SPIRITISTIC MEDIUM: A person under the direct influence or control of evil spirits who possesses occult powers.

SPIRITISTIC VISIONS / DREAMS - Visions leading to sensationalism which promote errant doctrines.

SPIRITUALIST or SPIRITIST: A person who believes in the ability to contact departed souls through a medium.

---

[6] Scott, Bryan, booklet Criss Angel "MindFreak", Titusville, FL, Center for Christian Counseling, 2006.

SPIRITUAL HIERARCHY OF MASTERS: New Age advocates believe these spiritual "masters" are highly evolved men who, having already perfected themselves, are now guiding the rest of humanity to this same end.

SPIRITS: Discarnate entities, often thought to be the spirits of ancestors, who are believed to influence the world of the living. In reality, fallen angels and demons are the "evil" spirits who are summoned during incantations.

SPIRITISM: Worship of or communication with the supposed spirits of the dead. These spirits are in reality evil spirits in disguise.

SPIRITUALISM: An ancient occult practice which teaches that the spirits of the deceased are alive to communicate with people here on Earth through "mediums" who act as intermediaries between the material world and the spirit world.

SPONDOMANCY: Finding omens in soot or cinders.

SPONTANEOUS PAST-LIFE RECALL: The process by which one is said to remember his/her past life without artificially induced means (i.e. hypnosis).

STAR GAZING / ASTROLOGY: The divination of the supposed influence of the stars upon human affairs and terrestrial events by their positions and aspects. Is. 47:12-15; Jer. 10:2.

STARS: Spiritual wisdom and development.

ST. JOHN"S EYE: The midsummer witch celebration; June 23.

STICHOMANCY: A form of Rhapsodomancy. See *Rhapsodomancy*

STOLISOMANCY: Observing oddities in a person's dress for omens.

STOLICTES: The neophyte grade of the Hermetic Order of the Golden Dawn.

SUBJECT: Person used for experiments in ESP studies.

SUCCUBUS (SUCCUBI): A female demonic force who copulates (sexual intercourse) with human males. See *Incubus*

SUFISM: Persian mystical religion based on Islam.

SUPERCONCIOUSNESS: That aspect of one's soul beyond the rational world of material reality that can achieve God-realization.

SUPERIORS: Junior mothers and fathers.

SUPERSTITION: Trust in magic or chance; a belief resulting from fear of the unknown.

SWEDENBORG, EMANUEL: 18th century son of a Lutheran minister, expounded supposed symbolic meaning of Scripture and developed such mediumistic abilities as astral projection and automatic writing and founded his own cult religion.

SYCOMANCY: Divination by writing possible responses to questions on tree leaves, and observing which one dries the fastest; a modern equivalent is to put responses on pieces of paper, roll them up, and place them in a strainer above a steaming pot to see which opens first.

SYLPH: An elemental who lives in air.

SYNCRETISM: Fusion of different forms of belief or practice; the claim that all religions are one and share the same core teachings.

SYNCHRONICITY: Meaningful coincides interpreted as having some higher, connecting purpose that could be accounted for by PSI phenomena.

SYNERGY: Quality of "whole making"; the New Age belief in the cooperation of natural systems to put things together in ever more meaningful patterns.

SYNTHESIS (in astrology): The interpretation of a complete astrological chart.

SYNTROPY: Belief that living matter has an inherent drive to perfect itself in increasingly complex patterns of association, communication, cooperation and awareness. The opposite of *Entropy*.

T

TABLE TILTING: The levitation or shifting of a table to help determine communication with the dead.

T'AI CHI: Chinese martial art of slow physical movements used with meditation to develop self-discipline and spiritual awareness; part of body work.

TALISMAN: A power object, usually an amulet or trinket.

TANTRA: Series of Hindu and Buddhist scriptures concerned with special yogic practices for swift attainment of enlightenment; also the practices, techniques, and traditions of these teachings.

TAOISM ("Dowism"): A Chinese religious philosophy founded in the sixth century B.C. by Lao-Tse, who taught that the "tao" or way of virtues is an eternal, all pervasive harmonizing force in the universe.

TARA CENTER: Non profit organization founded in 1980 by Benjamin Crème, dedicated to the p rinciple of internationally shared resources and the reappearance of the "Christ" in the person of Lord Iitreya.

TAROT CARDS: A set of 78 cards with illustrations into which are incorporated a vast amount of arcane symbolism. Considered by many to contain the sum total of all occult knowledge. The ancestor of our modern playing cards, the Tarot is today used primarily for divination (cartomancy). Playing cards with specially inscribed figures and emblems (such as the moon, sun, devil, and Egyptian god Isis) that are said to reveal the cosmic purpose of the universe and the future of each individual's life; a form of divination or fortune telling. Fortune telling by the manipulation and placing of cards which have certain meanings (e.g. the seven of hearts is a card of love.)

TASSEOGRAPHY: (See Tea Leaf Reading)

TAU MEGA THERION: A reference to the anti-Christ, literally means "the Great Beast". Appellation used by Aleister Crowley.

TEACUP READINGS: Interpreting the future by the arrangement of tea leaves in the bottom of a cup.

TEA-LEAF READING: An imprecise method of divination suggesting that the patterns formed by tea leaves left in the bottom of a cup reveal hidden truths about the subject in question.

TELEKINESIS: Movement of objects by occult power. A phenomenon that occurs when an object (table lifting or tumbler moving) is set in motion or a musical instrument is played without a visible or tangible cause.

TELEPATHY: The ability to communicate directly from mind to mind. Telepathy includes either the power to transmit thoughts to another person (words, symbols, images, ideas, sensations, or emotions), or the power of thought-reading or telepathic reception from another mind, and sometimes both.

TELEPORTATION: Instantaneous movement of a person or object form one place to another without going through normal space-time.

TEMPLE OF SET: A satanic organization founded by Dr. Michael Aquino. ("Set" is the Egyptian god of death)

TEPHRAMANCY: Divination by looking for messages in ashes, often burned tree bark.

THAUMATURGY: The use of magick to effect changes in the reality outside of the magician. The scientific and technical aspects of such workings. Also known as Sorcery.

THEOCENTRICITY: Belief that God is central to the propositions of man and omnipotent in his control of history's destiny.

THEOSOPHY: Literally, "Wisdom of God"; a religion incorporating some Christian concepts along with reincarnation, karma, and spiritistic practices.

THEOSOPHICAL SOCIETY: A highly developed system of occultism based on mystery religions and Hindu philosophy, founded on the writings of Helena Petrovna Lavatsky, a nineteenth-century Russian mystic; forerunner of much New Age thought.

THERAPEUTIC TOUCH: A form of spiritualistic healing asserting that properly passing hands over a patient's body, his "energy" can be properly distributed to bring health.

THEURGY: The use of magick to effect changes in the magician's own internal reality. Magick used for self-actualization or personal apotheosis. Focus is on prayers, invocations, medications.

THE WAY: Bringing about social change with three million people by 1990. They allegedly claim they will be in the White House. The Way appears to try to infiltrate law enforcement. They have a military group.

THIRD EYE: An occult concept assuming that a spiritually intuitive center of consciousness exists in the center of the forehead, the so-called seventh charka of enlightenment in yoga; hence the red dot in the forehead of Hindu women.

THOUGHT ADJUSTERS: In the cult Urantia, spirit guides that are "undiluted parts of Deity" and communicate with one's higher self.

THURIBLE: Also known as the witch's censer, the thurible holds incense that is used in ritual observances.

TIBETAN BOOK OF THE DEAD: Scriptures of Tibetan Buddhism based on esoteric experiences concerning the nature of the soul and the stages to be encountered during death.

TIROMANCY: A form of divination using cheese.

TOTEM: A species of plant or animal regarded as having an ancestral or affinitive relationship to a specific tribe, family, or individual.

TRANSCENDENTAL MEDITATION (TM): The Novice receives a Mantra, a special sound which he must keep secret. During meditation (which lasts for twenty minutes, twice each day), one must simply repeat the mantra mentally while ignoring all other thoughts. Regular meditation is supposed to let the mind descend to the deepest level of consciousness. The medit ator experiences full relaxation, renewed energy and creativity, and a sense of well being. TM is a religious system. The use of Mantras comes directly from the Hindu Yoga tradition and the "deepest level of consciousness" of which Maharishi speaks and seems to be identical with the ground of being, i.e. Brahman. For these reasons Maharishi can be considered a Guru. Those followers who discount his religious role are misguided at best.

TRANSMISSION: A method of spiritual communication forming an extradimensional entity that relays its messages through thought-to-thought transference or other mediumistic conveyances.

TRANSVECTION: Levitation, or the projection of a wraith form.

TRINITY (OCCULT STYLE): The triangle is the symbol of manifestation. It is here that the spirit will appear. A magician will do well to study the symbolism of the triangle and of the number three. Among other things, the triangle, represents the trinity, the triple nature of our world (mental, psychic, and physical), and the electromagnetic dynamism of the universe.

TRUMPET SPEAKING: Musical notes supposedly made by spirits through a special trumpet during a séance.

TRANCE: An altered state of consciousness, induced or spontaneous, that gives access to many ordinarily inhibited capacities of the mind-body system. Trance states are generally self-induced.

TRANCE CHANNELING: The phenomenon of a spirit's speaking through the mouth of a medium, or channeler, and often subjecting the channel to oblivion so that the channeler's neurosensory and psychomotor functions are completely possessed (through often mimicked by charlatans and fake channelers).

TRANSMIGRATION: The movement of the soul from one body to another. Transmigration is commonly used as broadly referring to reincarnations of many different types of life form, such as mineral, vegetative, and animal, as well as human.

TRANSPERSONAL PSYCHOLOGY: Technique for psychologically exploring the spiritual aspects of human nature; developed by Abraham Maslow.

TRANSFORMATION: New Age advocates promote both personal and planetary transformation. Personal transformation involves the changes wrought in one's life by increasing self-realization. As more and more people are personally transformed, the planet too will be transformed into a global brotherhood.

TRANSFERENCE: Evil spirits apparently leave the body or being of one individual, and enter into another. This sometimes happens at the choice of the individuals, at other times at the choice of the spirit. It frequently happens when a Christian is seeking deliverance for another person, and the spirit enters the would-be deliverer.

TISKELE OR TRISKELION: The tiskele is a symbol which appears in many logos today. Although the name may not be recognized by most people, they would recognize the symbol. "The triskelion (Greek for three legs) is a symbol of the sun intended to express motion. A similar device, with four legs, called a triskelion is a modification of the swastika." (Thomas Albert Stafford, <u>Christian Symbolism iln the Evangelical Churches</u>, Nashville, Tennessee, Abingdon Press, 1942. p. 75) The triskele is actually a Celtic version of the Yin-Yang symbol of life, and a modification of the swastika, so what we know about the yin/yang and the swastika applies to this symbol as well.

TRUMPET MEDIUM: A psychic or sensitive who brings forth "spirit voices" through a trumpet at séances.

U

UFO: Unidentified flying object; flying saucer. Frequently associated with the spirit world.

UMANDA (also see MACUMBA): Common in Brazil. Traces back to Africa plus Indian magic of the Americas, plus spiritistic elements, and some Catholic components. Headed by Cult Father, and Cult Mother. Mediums are sambas.

UNDINE: An elemental who lives in water.

UNITY: A cult that denies biblical doctrines of sin and salvation, yet uses Christian terminology to promote a unity of non-Christian/beliefs while claiming a reverence for Jesus as a great teacher; based on the teachings of Charles and Myrtle Fillmore, late 19th century spiritualists, who adapted the teachings of Christian Science and concluded that Jesus was merely a great teacher who acquired a "Christ-Consciousness" that we all can attain.

UNITY IN DIVERSITY COUNCIL: A New Age "metanetwork" of over 100 networks and groups rallying for global cooperation and interdependence.

UNIFIED FIELD THEORY: A concept of physics suggesting that an underlying principle guides all physical phenomena and is embodied in a single force that ensures stability and peace in the universe.

URANTIA FOUNDATION: Promotes psychic revelations and a cosmological view of the universe based on the 2,097-page "Urantia Book", supposedly dictated by extraterrestrial beings.

UROBOROS: A serpent depicted as eating his own tail; the symbol being used to show the unity of the sacrificer and the one sacrificed.

UPANISHADS: Philosophical literature by Indo-Aryans regarding the nature of ultimate truth and reality. The final section of the Vedas.

V

VAMPIRE: According to legend, one who rises from the grave by night to consume the blood of persons.

VAUDERIE (VAULDERIE): The witches' Sabbat.

VEDAS: The oldest Hindu scriptures, including a collection of hymns, and prose text on sacrificial rites and ceremonies, advice for the elderly retired, and the monistic philosophical speculations of the Upanishads. The main ideas are called Vedanta Hinduism.

VENFICA: A witch who uses poisons and philters.

VIBRATIONS: A magical aura or atmosphere.

VINNANA: In Buddhism, it is the "unconscious disposition" of the deceased which is reborn. It is not to be confused with the conscious self, soul, mind, etc.

VISUALIZATION: Attempts to manipulate reality through the mind.

VISUALIZATION HEALING: A form of New Age consciousness which intimates that the natural healing process of the body can be accelerated and activated by right thinking.

VOODOO: An ancient religion combining Catholicism and Sorcery. Those involved are extremely superstitious. Members use spells, sorcery, potions, and fetishes to control the actions of others or the outcome of events.

VOW: An earnest promise or pledge that binds one to perform a specific act or behave in a certain manner.

W

WALPURGIS NIGHT: The eve of May Day, believed in medieval Europe to be the occasion of a witch's sabbath. An episode or situation having the quality of nightmarish wildness associated with this sabbat (April 30).

WAND: Made of ash, willow or hazel, usually 21 inches long, plain or decorated priapic wand has an 8 or 9 inch phallus on one end.

WARLOCK: Originally meaning "one who breaks faith". It is more often used by non-witches to refer to a male witch. Actually designates a traitor.

WATCHER: A familiar acting as a guardian.

WATER WITCHING: See Dowsing.

WATER WITCHING or WATER DIVINING or WATER SMELLING: Locating water using a Divining Rod or other occult methods.

WAXING MOON: Changing Moon.

WEREWOLF: According to legend, a person who has been turned or turns himself into a wolf-like creature.

WHITE MAGIC: Used for blessing, or anything! Popularly, magick done for "good" purposes.

WICCA: An Old English word from which we get the word "witch". This is the paganistic end of the witchcraft spectrum. See *Wicca Appendix H*.

WINDHAM HILL: New Age music label started by two college dropouts who wanted to record and distribute solo instrumental music; thought to be the largest New Age music distributor.

WITCH: One who practices magic. Can produce magic alone or can be a member of a coven.

WITCH"S CORD OR GIRDLE: Also known as the cingulum, the witch's cord is used for ritualistic purposes.

WITCHCRAFT: The practice of sorcery or magic. The practice of the old religion which focuses on the goddess in her many forms: Hectate, Aphrodite, Astarte, Diana. Women play important roles in witchcraft.

WITCH'S SABBATH: Meeting of a witches' coven held in order to perform magical rites and ceremonies. A large number of witches and warlocks who would gather around a bonfire or cauldron, light black candles, and perform sacrifices. The Sabbath would culminate in a sexual orgy.

WITNESS: Student minister.

WIZARD: One skilled in magic, sorcerer; male witch .

WIZARDRY: The art of practices of a wizard; sorcery.

WRAITH: A projected astral body or mobile form of witch power.

WORLD GOODWILL: A New Age political lobby that aims to unfold "the Plan" as spelled out in the writings of Alice Bailey.

WORLD HEALING MEDITATION: A December 31, 1986 gathering of New Agers to mediate for peace under the inspirational tutelage of John Price.

WORLD VIEW: A common consensus about the nature of reality; a set of presuppositions or premises held consciously or unconsciously about the makeup of the cosmos.

X

XYLOMANCY: Divination using pieces of wood, either by interpreting their shape or noting the order in which they burn in a fire.

Y

YAHWEH (sect): Allegedly black Hebrew Israelite. Originally headquartered in Miami and have an alleged branch in Tampa. It appears that their philosophy is a black supremacy philosophy. Their mode of dress is Biblical garb. (They have been identified in other areas of the United States).

YANG: The male force.

YANTRA: The visual equivalent of a mantra, supposing that a meditative state can be induced by staring at a colorful diagram of concentric or geometric design.

YELLOW MAGIC: Used for mental work, meditation, etc. Intellect.

YIN YANG: Chinese names referring to the active and passive principles of the universe. Yin refers to the female or (inactive) negative force; Yang to the male or active force. These two polar forces continually interplay with each other. The words are used to describe the constant flow of motion and change in the universe (i.e. the "Tao"). Known as "chi" force.

YIN: The female force.

YOGA: Literally, "yoking" or "joining"; any system or spiritual discipline by which the practitioner or Yogi seeks to condition the self at all levels-physical, psychical, and spiritual. The goal of the Indian religious tradition is a state of well-being, the loss of self-identity, and absorption into union with the Absolute, or Ultimate Being. The rising popularity of *Hatha-Yoga* in the Western world warrants a discussion of the practice of Yoga as a dangerous form of occultism. See *Hatha Yoga Appendix I*.

YOGI: Master of one or more methods of Yoga who teaches it to others.

YULE: A midwinter witch festival, occult Holiday, Winter Solstice, December 22, the shortest day of the year.

Z

ZEN: Two-branched type of Buddhism thought best known for its emphasis on an experience of enlightenment that occurs from breaking down the commitment and attachment to the logical and rational ordering of experience.

ZODIAC: Imaginary belt in the heavens that encompasses the apparent paths of the principal planets for Pluto. Divided into twelve constellations or signs based on the assumed dates that the sun enters each of these "houses" or symbols, the Zodiac is used for predictions in Astrology.

ZOMBIE: In actuality, one who has been deliberately poisoned with puffer fish venom and thought to be dead when body functions slow and become unrecognizable. Often they are buried by the family after which the perpetrator removes the body and revives the individual in a disorientated state by forcing ingestion of jumson weed combined with hypnosis.

ZONE THERAPY: The philosophical basis for such practices as reflexology and iridology, which supposes that certain zones of the body can give "a picture" or "connect" with symptoms of disease in other, unrelated portions of the body.

ZOOLATRY: Worship of animals.

Appendix

Appendix A

Freemasonry

Freemasonry: An Indictment of the Church

Freemasonry is an open indictment against the Christian Church in America because it is so widely accepted among those who believe in Jesus Christ as their Savior. Although they profess faith in Christ, these people turn from Jesus, the Light of the world, to seek more so-called "light" as they approach the "Worshipful Master in the east," Freemasonry's representative for the rising sun.

Freemasonry is an indictment against the Christian Church because it indicates the Church's gross lack of spiritual insight and discernment. In 1 Corinthians 2:15 Paul said that "the spiritual man makes judgments about all things." Yet, the Church has not apprehended the true nature of Freemasonry's idolatrous system. The Church largely embraces Masonry as a social and ethical institution advocating high moral standards for its adherents. Many look upon Masonry as synonymous with Christianity. As we will discover in this section, Freemasonry is in no way equivalent to Christianity, and neither are its morals or ethics.

It is our prayer that no individual Mason will be offended by this work. Our effort here is not directed to the individual Mason, rather to the Masonic system itself.

We are approaching this subject with questions and answers. Each question is deliberately designed to teach some aspect of the Masonic philosophy, ritual and ceremony.

The History of Freemasonry

Freemasonry is an oath-bound fraternity which began in England, not in Palestine, Egypt, Greece, or Rome as some have suggested. The first lodge whose records survive starts its documentation in 1701; however, Scotland had lodges in the 16th century. The stonemasons of England and Scotland had developed certain organizations such as the lodge, which seems to have taken its basic form in the 14th and 15th centuries. These organizations or lodges arose to meet the needs of the craft whose members were often itinerant masons. They assembled for fellowship and mutual help. The lodge organization aided in the enforcement of the codes of discipline within the craft and helped to preserve secrecy about the trade's practices. There gradually evolved a secret ritual, as well as a system of signals for mutual recognition of its members. Legends later grew up concerning the supposed ancient origin of the society, the most common version perhaps being that which traces their beginnings to Hiram, the master-mason and builder of Solomon's Temple (1 Kings 5-6). This inaccurate legend claims that Hiram was murdered because he refused to reveal the mason's secrets.

The first annual meeting of the Grand Lodge was held in London in 1717. Benjamin Franklin was a member of the first unchartered lodge in America which was located in Philadelphia. The first chartered lodge in this country was located in Boston, Massachusetts in 1733, and was called the "First Lodge." Several early Americans were Freemasons, including George Washington, Alexander Hamilton, Paul Revere, Admiral John Paul Jones, and nine of the signers of the Declaration of Independence. At least thirteen United States Presidents have been Freemasons, and many contemporary political leaders are members of the organization, including cabinet members, Supreme Court justices, senators, representatives, state governors, and congressmen. It is reported that in the United States there are over 15,000 lodges and 49 Grand Lodges with 4,000,000 members. Britain has some 750,000 Freemasons, and over a million more are found throughout the rest of the world.

Three basic degrees are offered in Freemasonry: Entered Apprentice, Fellow-Craft, and Master Mason. There are also a variety of higher degrees for those who can attain them. Various bodies have different names, such as Craft Rite, Knights Templar, Scottish Rite, Shrine Temple, and so on. There are also women's orders, such as Order of the Eastern Star, White Shrine, and Daughters of the Nile.

According to the Highest Masonic Authority, What is Freemasonry?

According to Freemasonry's highest Masonic authority, Prince Adept Albert Pike, "Masonry is a search for Light. That search leads us directly back, as you see, to the Kabalah (Jewish Book of Magic). In that ancient and little understood medley of absurdity and philosophy, the Initiate will find the source of many doctrines; and many in time come to understand the Hermetic philosophers, the Alchemist, all the Anti-papal Thinkers of the Middle Ages, and Emanuel Swedenborg." (*Morals and Dogma of the Ancient and Accepted Scottish Rite of Masonry*, p. 741)

Does Freemasonry Foster or Emphasize a Specific Religion? Is it not Actually a Religious Institution?

Dr. Albert G. Mackey claims, "The truth is, Masonry is undoubtedly a religious institution" (*Textbook of Masonic Jurisprudence,* p. 95). Again, Dr. Mackey explains "As Masons we are taught never to commence any great or important undertaking without first invoking the blessing and protection of deity, and this is because Masonry is a religious institution." (*Manual of the Lodge,* p. 40)

What Kind of Religion is Freemasonry?

Dr. Mackey reveals, "The religion then of Masonry is pure theism on which its different members engraft their peculiar opinions, but they are not permitted to introduce them into the lodge or to connect their truth or falsehood with the truth of Masonry." (*Lexicon of Freemasonry,* p. 404)

Dr. J.D. Buck MD, 32nd degree, says, "Masonry is not only a universal science, but a world wide religion, and owes allegiance to no one creed, and can adopt no such sectarian dogma as such, without ceasing thereby to be Masonic...that "Masonry is the universal religion only because and only so long as it embraces all religions." (*Mystic Masonry,* pp. 113-114)

Robert Morris proudly proclaims, "So broad is the religion of Masonry, and so carefully are all sectarian tenets excluded from the system, that the Christian, the Jew, and the Mohammedan, in all their numberless sects and divisions, may, and do harmoniously combine in its moral and intellectual work with the Buddhist, the Parsee, the Confucian, and the worshipper of Deity under any form." (*Webb's Monitor of Freemasonry,* p. 280)

Does Freemasonry have a Priest?

Robert Morris defines "chaplain" in this way: "The Master of the Lodge is its priest, and director of its religious ceremonies. His duty is to select the Scriptures, prayers, etc., and he should be present at the burial of the dead." (*Webb's Monitor of Freemasonry,* p. 231)

Is Freemasonry a Christian Institution?

Dr. Albert G. Mackey clearly states, "Freemasonry is not Christianity, nor a substitute for it." (*Encyclopedia of Freemasonry,* p. 162)

What is a Masonic Lodge?

According to Albert Pike, "Every Masonic Lodge is a temple of religion; and its teachings are institutions in religion." (*Morals & Dogma,* p. 213)

Is Freemasonry Based on the Bible?

We find this statement on the subject: "Masonry has nothing whatsoever to do with the Bible, that it is not founded on the Bible, for if it were it would not be Masonry, it would be something else." (*Digest of Masonic Law,* pp. 207-209)

Again according to Albert Pike, "The Bible is an indispensable part of the furniture of a Christian Lodge, only because it is the sacred book of the Christian religion. The Hebrew Pentateuch in a Hebrew Lodge, and the Koran in the Mohammedan one, belong on the altar; and one of these, and the square and Compass, properly understood, are the great lights by which a Mason must walk." (*Morals and Dogma,* p.11)

Which of These Furnishings
Does Freemasonry Esteem the Least?

The Bible! Because according to Mr. Pike's answer to the previous question, the Bible only appears with the Square and Compass in so-called Christian lodges, while the Square and Compass must appear in every Lodge.

Is the Name of God and His Son Jesus Reverenced Among Masons?

In the Masonic Handbook, p. 184, we discover, "Whether you swear or take God's name in vain don't matter so much. Of course the name of the Lord Jesus Christ, as you know, don't amount to anything, but Mah-hah-bone – O, horror! You must never, on any account, speak that awful name aloud. That would be a most heinous crime – unmasonic – unpardonable."

Does Freemasonry Equate Jesus Christ with the Sun-god of Hinduism, Krishna?

J.D. Buck makes this declaration, "It has been shown that every act in the drama of the life of Jesus, and every quality assigned to Christ, is to be found in the life of Krishna." (*Mystic Masonry,* pp. 119, 138)

Is a Christian Allowed to Witness in a Masonic Lodge Concerning Christ's Redemptive Work?

Dr. Albert G. Mackey admonishes, "A Christian Mason is not permitted to introduce his own peculiar opinions with regards to Christ's meditorial office into the lodge." (*Lexicon of Freemasonry,* p. 404)

Does Freemasonry Offer Its Candidates Regeneration, or the New-birth, without Jesus Christ?

Daniel Sickles explains, "The Rite of Induction signifies the end of a profane and vicious life, the palingenesia (new-birth) of corrupt human nature the death of vice and all bad passions and the introduction to the new life of purity and virtue." (*Ahiman Rezon,* p. 54)

Does Freemasonry Promise Life After Death Without Jesus Christ?

Daniel Sickles claims, "If we with suitable true devotion maintain our Masonic profession, our faith will become a beam of light and bring us to those blessed mansions where we shall be eternally happy with God, the Great Architect of the Universe." (*Ahiman Rezon,* p. 79)

How Does a Mason Obtain Freedom From Sin?

According to Albert G. Mackey, an Acacian is a term signifying a Mason who by living in strict obedience to the obligations and precepts of the fraternity is free from sin." (*Lexicon of Freemasonry,* p. 16)

Does Freemasonry Mutilate the Scriptures to Suit Its own Purposes?

Yes! On page 31 of the <u>Royal Arch Degree Charge at Opening</u>, an edited version of the following verse of Scripture is read: "Now we command you, brethren, **in the name of the Lord Jesus Christ** that ye withdraw yourselves from every brother that walketh disorderly, and not after the tradition which ye received from us." (2 Thess. 3:6)

The portion in bold in the verse above is omitted by Freemasonry and for a very obvious reason: the name of Jesus is not permitted in the Lodge.

Are Ministers Forbidden to Pray in the Name of the Lord Jesus Christ in a Masonic Lodge?

In the Masonic Handbook, p. 74, we find: "When a brother reveals any of our great secrets; whenever, for instance, he tells anything about Boaz, or Tubalcain, or Jachin, or that awful Mah-hah-bone, or even whenever a minister prays in the name of Christ in any of our assemblies, you must always hold yourself in readiness, if called upon, to cut his throat from ear to ear, pull out his tongue by the roots, and bury his body at the bottom of some lake or pond."

Has such a Horrible Thing ever been Done Among Masons?

We will continue the preceding quotation as follows: "Of course, all this (the cutting of the throat and burying in some lake or pond) must be done in secret, as it was the case of that notorious man Morgan, for both law and civilization are opposed to such barbarous crimes, but then, you know you must live up to your obligation, and so long as you have sworn to do it, by being very strict and obedient in the matter, you'll be free from sin." (*Masonic Handbook,* p. 74)

NOTE: Captain William Morgan, a Mason of some thirty years, took it upon himself to expose what he knew of Masonry. He wrote his manuscript Freemasonry Exposed, and was allegedly murdered, in the opinion of all who have carefully examined the evidence. The Masonic Handbook at least intimates that this was the case.

Are Masons Truthful?

if you live up to your obligation strictly, you'll be free from sin." (*Masonic Handbook,* p. 183) In the Masonic Handbook we read: "If your wife, or child, or a friend, should ask you anything about your initiation – as, for instance, if your clothes were taken off, if you were blindfolded, if you had a rope around your neck, etc., you must conceal...hence, of course, you must deliberately lie about it. It is part of your obligation, nevertheless. But you know if you live in strict obedience to your obligation, you'll be free from sin." (p. 74)

Again we find, "You must conceal all the crimes of your brother Masons, except murder and treason, and these only at your own option, and should you be summoned as a witness against a brother Mason be always sure to shield him. Prevaricate, don't tell the whole truth in this case, keep his secrets, forget the most important points. It may be perjury to do this, it is true, but you're keeping your obligations, and remember

Are Masons Ethical?

The <u>Masonic Handbook</u> clearly states, "Whenever you see any of our signs made by a brother Mason, and especially the grand hailing sign of distress, you must always be sure to obey them, even at the risk of your life. If you're on a jury, and the defendant is a Mason, and makes the Grand Hailing sign, you must obey it; you must disagree with your brother jurors, if necessary, but you must be sure not to bring the Mason guilty, for that would bring disgrace upon our order. It may be perjury, to be sure, to do this, but then your fulfilling your obligation, and you know if you live up to your obligations you'll be free from sin." (p. 183)

Are Masons Honest?

Again the <u>Masonic Handbook</u> reveals, "If you cheat, wrong, or defraud any other society or individual, it is entirely your own business. If you cheat the Government even, Masonry cannot and will not touch you, but be careful not to cheat, wrong, or defraud a brother Mason or a lodge, whoever else you may defraud; live up to your obligation, and you'll be free from sin." (p. 184)

Do Masons have the Well Being of all Men at Heart, or only Their Fellow Masons?

The <u>Masonic Handbook</u> further explains, "Whether you quarrel with or strike other men is none of our business, but your obligations enjoin you not to strike a brother Master Mason. It may be wicked and sinful, to be sure, to strike any man, or to quarrel with anybody, but our rules make no provision except for the protection of Masons only, and if you live in strict obedience to your obligation, you'll be free from sin." (p. 184)

Are Masons Taught that Moral Chastity be Practiced Among all Peoples, or Among the Families of Master Masons only?

The "Chastity Covenant" of the Master Mason states, "Furthermore, that I will not violate the chastity of a Master Mason's wife, mother, sister, or daughter, knowing them to be such. This gives you full permission, my dear sir, to do as you please outside of the Masonic order, but you must always respect the female relatives of Masons." (*Masonic Handbook, p. 184*)

Why Are Masons Taught Temperance?

The drinking of alcoholic beverages is synonymous with the activities of the "Mystic Shrine;" yet, Masons are taught temperance. Why?

Daniel Sickles explains, "The chief aim and the essence of these virtues is to keep safely the secrets of Masonry. Temperance is enjoined, not for its own sake, but for the reason that when a Mason is intoxicated, he might unwittingly reveal the secrets of Masonry." (*Ahiman Rezon,* p. 96)

Is Masonry Kind and Benevolent?

Mr. Edmond Ronayne, Past Master of Keystone Lodge No. 639, Chicago, Ill., claims, "All my experience in and out of Masonic Lodges, has gone to establish the fact in my mind that Freemasonry in all its departments is the most corrupt and wicked, and contains the greatest amount of falsehood of any other institution on the face of the globe. . . It is positively and absolutely selfish in every single element of its pagan composition, and can truthfully lay no more claim to charity, benevolence or goodness of any other name or description than could say of the heathen organizations which Christian civilization has long since banished from the world." (*Master's Carpet,* p. 38)

(Author's Note on Morals and Ethics)

We question the morals and ethics of this supposedly benevolent and highly moral fraternity, because according to its own claims, it is only moral or ethical in respect to its own members. This is due to the fact that Masons are not subject to the law of God, but to their own law, the universal law of nature. Temperance is taught in Masonry, but not for the physical or spiritual well being of the adherent, but to keep safely the secrets of Masonry.

Oaths and Obligations

In Pierson's Traditions of Freemasonry we read: "A solemn method of confirming an oath i.e. in the 'Mysteries,' was by placing a drawn sword across the throat of the person to whom it was administered, and invoking heaven, earth and sea to witness the ratification. Among the Druids it was a necessary duty of the bards to unsheath the sword against those who had forfeited their obligation by divulging any of the secrets of the order." (p. 35)

First or Entered Apprentice Degree

"I do most solemnly and sincerely promise and swear, without the least equivocation, mental reservation, or self evasion of mind in me whatever; binding myself under no less penalty than to have my throat cut across, my tongue torn out by the roots, and my body buried in the rough sands of the sea at low watermark, where the tide ebbs and flows twice in twenty-four hours; so help me God, and keep me steadfast in the due performance of the same."

Second or Fellow Craft Degree:

"I do most solemnly and sincerely promise and swear without the least hesitation, mental reservation, or self evasion of mind in me whatever; binding myself under no less penalty than to have my left breast torn open and my heart and vitals taken from thence and thrown over my left shoulder and carried into the valley of Jehosaphat, there to become a prey to wild beasts of the field, and vulture of the air, if ever I should prove willfully guilty of violating any part of this my solemn oath or obligation of a Fellow Craft Mason so help me God, and keep me steadfast in the due performance of the same."

Third or Master's Degree:

I do solemnly promise and swear, with a fixed and steady purpose of mind in me to keep and perform the same, binding myself under no less penalty than to have my body severed in two in the midst, and divided to the north and south, and my bowels burnt to ashes in the center, and the ashes scattered before the four winds of heaven, that there might not the least track or trace of remembrance remain among men, or Masons, of so vile and perjured a wretch as I should be, were I ever to prove willfully guilty of violating any part of this my solemn oath or obligation of a Master Mason. So help me God, and keep me steadfast in the due performance of the same."

(Author's Note on Oath Taking)

In each of the first degrees the candidate is brought from the preparation room with a rope or "cable tow" around his neck. In the second degree the cable tow is around his right shoulder, and in the third degree the cable tow is around his waist. The symbolism of this rope cable tow is very simple: the candidate is bound with the rope until he is bound with the oath. Once he is bound by an invisible rope of fear, the little blue rope is no longer needed.

We question just what kind of god would listen to such horrible and barbarous oaths as those sworn by Masonic candidates? Surely it is not the God of the Bible. The oaths would be much more suitable as oaths to Satan, the god of this world.

Does the God of the Bible take these oaths seriously? God considers spoken vows so important that the Bible advises against taking oaths (Ecclesiastes 5:2-6, Matthew 5:33-37, James 5:12). Although the God of the Bible would never require keeping such horrendous oaths as those imposed by Freemasonry on its followers, these oaths made to other gods are a serious indication of the idolatry inherent in the Masonic religion.

Does Freemasonry Believe in the Personal God of the Scriptures?

No! In J.D. Buck's Mystic Masonry, p. 216, we read concerning the personality of God: "The only personal God Freemasonry accepts is 'humanity in toto.' God (the Great Architect of the Universe) personifies himself, that is expresses that potency of himself which personality is, through man. Humanity therefore is the only personal god that there is."

To What Other Deities might Freemasonry's Great Architect be Compared?

Freemasonry's Prince Adept Albert Pike says, "It is but an old term revived. Our adversaries numerous and formidable as they are, will say and will have a right to say that our Creative Principle is identical with the Generative Principle of the Indian and Egyptian, and may fitly be symbolized as it was symbolized anciently by the linga (penis)." (Blavatsky's *Isis Unveiled*, vol. 2, p. 377)

Martin L. Wagner observes, "From what we have learned in our study of freemasonry, it is this creative or generative principle that it worships as its specific god, and if this is true, then according to the testimony of Mr. Pike, the greatest of Masons, Masonry has abandoned the worship of Jehovah, and is simply wallowing in the styes of Paganism." (*Interpretation of Freemasonry*, p. 74)

(Author's Note on the god of Freemasonry)

Freemasonry like all other religions has its own revelation, the revelation of visible nature. Freemasonry's deity is not the God of the Bible, but a generative or creative principle synonymous with the Creative Principle of the Indian and Egyptian.

What is the Sin of Freemasonry?

The great sin of Freemasonry is idolatry! *"Although they claimed to be wise, they became fools and exchanged the glory of the immortal God for images made to look like mortal man and birds and animals and reptiles...They exchanged the truth of God for a lie, and worshipped and served created things rather than the Creator – who is forever praised, Amen."* Romans 1:22,23,25

Conclusion

Sufficient evidence has been presented to convince any person of a sincere spirit that the god of Freemasonry is not the great God of the Universe who created the heavens and the earth, but the god of this world, Satan. It offers a lost sinner a way to heaven without the God of the Bible, the Lord Jesus Christ, or the Church.

So very little of Freemasonry has been questioned by its adherents, yet so very much has been revealed by its literature. It is obvious that no professing Christian should ever be a part of Freemasonry.

Appendix B

Halloween

When we were kids growing up, we always looked forward to Halloween. We knew nothing about how it began, or what the meanings were behind it. All we knew was that we could get dressed up funny and go through our Cincinnati neighborhood knocking on doors for either candy or money. In fact, the night before Halloween was penny night when we would go out and collect pennies at each home.

The information in this section will help you understand the seriousness of Halloween. It is not to spoil children's fun, but to ask the question: Should we, as Christians, join in a festival whose history and practices are pagan and evil? Today, Halloween is a billion dollar business second only to Christmas in retailing, but few understand the true nature and historic foundations of this occult celebration.

Origin of Halloween

The word "Halloween" actually has its origins in the Catholic Church. It comes from the words "All Hallows Eve," "All Hallows Day," or "All Saints Day." This day was set aside to honor saints. The holiday was founded to try to divert attention away from the pagan practices taking place on this day each October. Although well intended, trying to "Christianize" pagan practices can never be pleasing to God, and Halloween may be the most vivid example of this. Some believe Irish immigrants fleeing the potato famine may have brought its origins to America in the 1840's.

In occult and witchcraft circles, October 31 represents a day of worship called Samhain (pronounced *sow-en*). This is the Celtic New Year. History testifies that the Celtic people were worshipers of earth gods, woodland spirits, and sun deities. One legend explains that on Samhain the spirits of all those who had died throughout the year would come back in search of living bodies to possess for the next year. It was believed to be their only hope for entering the afterlife. It was also the day that the living were to communicate with the dead. This practice is called necromancy.

Deuteronomy 18:11 tells us that God considers this practice evil. We see examples of necromancy portrayed in movies like *The Sixth Sense, Lion King,* and *Ghost,* to name a few. Regardless of where or how the ritual practice started, one thing is certain - God forbids contacting any spirit unless it's the *Holy Spirit!*

Symbols of Halloween

Trick or Treat. Here are three of the possible origins of present day "trick or treating":

a. In the early practice of Halloween, people were afraid of spirits doing harm to their home, so they would leave treats out side their homes to keep them happy.

b. The Europeans tried to "Christianize" this pagan ritual by calling it "souling." They would go out and collect soul cakes. The more cakes you would receive, the more prayers you would send up for your dead relatives. Similar to prayers for dead relatives in Catholicism.

c. In celebration of the recently completed harvest, Celts would give offerings of food to the gods. They often went from door to door to collect food to donate to their deities. History tells us that on Halloween the Celts would terrorize the countryside and populace, butcher cattle, and take it as spoil to please their gods

Today's trick-or-treating consists of going from house to house and receiving candy from all the neighbors. Even if Halloween were totally harmless and free from pagan tradition, I would still be concerned about taking my children door-to-door and taking candy from people that I may not know. Throughout the rest of the year, we teach our children not to take anything from a stranger. But on Halloween we break our own rules!!!

The Jack o'Lantern. The Celts who lived in what is now Great Britain and northern France would carry a lantern when they walked on the eve of October 31. These lanterns were carved out of big turnips and the lights were believed to keep the evil spirits away. Children carved faces in the turnips calling them "jack o'lanterns." People later started to use the pumpkin in order to carry a bigger light.

The myth behind the jack o'lantern was that a man named Jack made a pact with the Devil and had to wander aimlessly through the darkness with only a piece of coal from hell in a turnip to guide him.

There are many people who believe a person can never become a Christian once they have made a pact with the devil. This isn't true as the Bible says in John 8:44a in reference to all humanity prior to accepting Christ as Savior: "You belong to your father, the devil, and you want to carry out your father's desire."

But trusting Jesus as their Savior *sets men free!* So, why would the Devil make a deal with someone when they are already his? When an individual calls on God to forgive them and trusts Jesus as Savior, no matter what the past, God will hear and forgive.

Witches. When we were growing up, we were always told that witches were make-believe. But, witches are real. The Bible talks about them in several passages.

Today witchcraft is a very popular religion among our youth in America. Who would have ever thought that a seventeen-year-old honor student in Detroit, Michigan, could sue her school for the right to wear her pentagram, which is a symbol of her Wiccan religion. This is exactly what Crystal Seifferly did, according to the *Chicago Tribune,* February 10, 1999.

The Wiccan religion does not believe in the Devil or Satan. They believe in five elementals, which are the false gods of forces. The five elementals are earth, wind, fire, water, and spirits. Witches do not claim to be Devil worshippers. Witches do not believe the Bible is true so they will not accept a character from the Bible to worship. Many witches will hide behind environmentalism as a cover-up for the worship of Gaia, the goddess called "Mother earth."

The Black Cat. The black cat has long been associated with witchcraft. Many superstitions have evolved about cats. It was believed that witches could change into cats. Some people also believe that cats were the spirits of the dead. Friends and relatives who had died would often return, with their souls inhabiting an animal - often a black cat. Black cats have remained a symbol of Halloween to the present. On the eve before their New Year (October 31), it was believed that Samhain called together all the deceased. The dead would take different forms, with the evil spirits taking the form of animals - the most wicked taking the form of cats.

The belief of people coming back from the dead is *not* a Christian belief. That belief is called reincarnation. The Bible teaches that man dies only once. "Just as man is destined to die once, and after that to face judgment." (Hebrews 9:27).

Dressing in Costumes. During the festival of Samhain, there was a fire festival to honor the god of death. Sacred bonfires were lit on the tops of hills in honor of the false gods. History tells us that after the bonfire to Samhain, people were afraid to walk home in the dark. They were in fear of being possessed by spirits. So they dressed up in costumes and carved scary faces in their fire holders. They hoped that the spirits would be frightened and not bother them.

Without even knowing it, children in our society today continue this pagan practice by dressing up in various costumes. Pumpkins are now the objects of choice to carve faces into. The wearing of death masks is still used around the world in certain ceremonies when worshipping the spirits..

In Conclusion

In Deuteronomy 18:10-12, God gave His people **nine** things they were to stay away from. Many of the practices go hand in hand with the traditions of Halloween and go directly **against** God's Word.

1. **Human sacrifice**: In ancient times, they would offer children to false gods of fire. The bonfire was used by pagans who worshipped fire gods, like Baal. To appease these gods, they would offer children in the fire.

2. **Divination/fortune telling**: If you watch much TV, you can't miss the advertisements of psychics and people who are suppose to know your future. This practice is condemned in the Bible.

3. **Observer of times**: This is astrology. Christians do not believe that the stars can guide their life. Christians believe that God will guide our lives through His Word.

4. **Enchanter**: A person who uses chants to cast spel

5. **Witch**: Witches are not make-believe characters. Exodus 22:18 says: "Thou shalt not suffer a witch to live." Though New Testament Christians certainly do not condone the Old Testament practice of executing witches, the fact is they have become accepted members in our culture today.

6. **Charmer**: Objects that are made by someone to protect you or curse others.

7. **Consulter of familiar spirits**: a familiar spirit is a spirit that impersonates a person who is dead.

8. **A wizard, magician, or sorcerer**: a person who uses magic to control people or uses occult practices to entice people into witchcraft.

9. **Necromancer**: someone who claims to contact the dead.

Deuteronomy 18:10-12 says:

Let no one be found among you who sacrifices his son or daughter in the fire, who practices divination or sorcery, interprets omens, engages in witchcraft, or casts spells, or who is a medium or spiritist or who consults with the dead. Anyone who does these things is detestable to the Lord, and because of these detestable practices the Lord your God will drive out those nations before you.

Another question needs to be asked: What should be done with those things a Christian might have in their life that are associated with witchcraft? Acts 19:18-20 gives the answer: *Many of those who believed now came and openly confessed their evil deeds. A number who had practiced sorcery brought their scrolls together and burned them publicly. When they calculated the value of the scrolls, the total came to fifty thousand drachmas. In this way the word of the Lord spread widely and grew in power.*

So, what is the answer to our opening question - should a Christian be involved with the pagan holiday of Halloween? No! Ephesians 5:11 says, **Have nothing to do with the fruitless deeds of darkness, but rather expose them.** Not only should a Christian not partake in evil, *we are to expose it!*

A final point to consider is that if there is any single thing Christians need to do on October 31st it is to pray! This is the highest unholy day for those in the occult. Witches believe that the separation between the natural and spiritual worlds is thinnest during this day, so the amount of evil supernatural activity is going to be greatest that day. Also, it is known that more sacrifice (animal and human) is carried out on October 31st than on all the other days of the year combined. Christians should be praying and conducting spiritual warfare against the powers of darkness! Along with Christ-centered activities for our children, churches should consider some teaching from the above information followed by a time of prayer, binding the forces of darkness and asking God to protect our neighborhoods, cities and citizens.

Appendix C

Illinois State Law #87-1167
Ritualized Abuse of a Child

The State of Illinois, Public Act #87-1167, Effective January 1, 1993. Be it Enacted by the Legislature of the State of Illinois RITUALIZED ABUSE OF A CHILD-EXCLUSIONS-PENALTIES-DEFINITION.

(a) A person is guilty of a felony when he commits any of the following acts with, upon, or in the presence of a child as part of a ceremony, rite, or similar observance.

(1) **Actually** or in simulation, tortures, mutilates, or **sacrifices** any warm-blooded animal or **human being**;

(2) Forces injection, ingestion, or other application of any narcotic drug, hallucinogen or anesthetic for the purpose of dulling sensitivity, cognition, recollection of, or resistance to any criminal activity:

(3) Forces ingestion or external application of human or animal urine, feces, flesh, blood, bones, body secretions, non-prescribed drugs or chemical compounds.

(4) **Involves a child** in a mock, unauthorized or **unlawful marriage ceremony** with another person or **representation of any force or deity, followed by sexual contact with the child;**

(5) Places a living child into a coffin or open grave containing a human corpse or remains;

(6) Threatens death or serious harm to a child, his or her parents, family, pets, or friends which instills a well-founded fear in the child that the threat will be carried out, or;

(7) Unlawfully dissects, mutilates or incinerates a human corpse.

(Bold print added by author)

Appendix D

Reiki

In the *Encyclopedia of Alternative Health Care,* author Kristin Olsen says Reiki is "an energy healing system based on ancient Tibetan knowledge discovered by a Japanese theologian." Many people have commented on the ecumenical aspect of Reiki. Supposedly it was founded by Dr. Mikao Usui, a Japanese Christian minister in Kyoto, Japan, in the mid-1800's. When one of his students challenged his belief that Jesus Christ healed people with His hands, Dr Usui began a quest for proof that this type of healing actually did exist.

When he was unable to find the answers he looked for in the Bible, Usui set out to learn the ancient language of Sanskrit and then began to read the sutras, the ancient books of esoteric Hindu religious teachings. After completing years of study and meditation, Usui came upon what to him was a healing knowledge he termed "Reiki." This name comes from the Japanese words *rei,* meaning "boundless and universal," and *ki,* meaning "vital life energy force that flows through all living beings."

We are told that after Usui discovered this healing in the sutras, he undertook a three week fast atop a mountain in Japan. On the last day of his meditative quest, he reported that a ball of light containing the symbols of what later would become Reiki hit him on the forehead. This new power proved itself to Usui when he stubbed his toe as he came down the mountain after the fast. His toe, so he claimed, was immediately healed with his new energy healing system.

Today Reiki is an energy technique that is passed from Reiki masters to initiates. According to Olsen, these Reiki masters themselves don't understand how it works. They can only describe it as a linking with the cosmic radiant energy, an opening of chakras, or an attunement with universal life energy.

Olsen is struck by the similarities between the empowerment rituals of Tibetan Buddhism and the Reiki initiation ceremony. She describes it as a modern secular adaptation of ancient sacred knowledge used in healing and self-healing

How Reiki Works

The Reiki treatments consist of a series of usually three or four sessions lasting about one hour each. The practitioner's hands are held at twelve basic positions for five minutes each. Although there are many possible hand positions, a practitioner allows his or her own intuition to guide the placing. Over problem areas the holding time is doubled. During a Reiki session the practitioner supposedly draws energy and focuses it through his hands, thus providing a link between himself and the patient. Some Reiki teachers have described this connection as "lighting up."

Proponents say this technique can be applied to the practitioner himself, to other people, to plants, or to animals. Reiki practitioners say they can even heal long distance! They do not claim to diagnose or to possess medical skills. But with practice they claim to be able to detect energy responses from the body that often give clues to the site of the organic problem and its seriousness.

What are the spiritual aspects?

Reiki practitioners staunchly deny that what they do has anything to do with religion or God. The Reiki master is not a guru, they insist. However, it is difficult not to notice the channeling of universal energy which is the very basis of the Hindu prana and other energy manipulating techniques. There are definite spiritual aspects to this practice.

Evidence of Reiki healing relies on stories and testimonies. Often these are full of unexpected effects and cures.

As with so many other questionable practices, Reiki is couched in medical disclaimers. A Reiki teacher named Michael O'Leary is quoted in the *Encyclopedia of Alternative Health Care* as saying this energy work can help the terminally ill, but "not so much to cure the cancer, because sometimes there is just not enough wholeness to expand to sustain physical life."

Needless to say, this questionable therapy is one that needs to be avoided.

Appendix E

Harry Potter

Harry Potter is a fantasy novel series written by J.K. Rowling. Currently there are six books in the series. The books detail Harry's mystical adventures as a wizard in training at Hogwart's School of Witchcraft & Wizardry. As of January 2001 the craze over Harry Potter had put 90 million books in print in over 43 languages in 200 countries. Think how those numbers have grown in the past years. Unfortunately these books have been praised by some evangelical leaders who have failed to understand the deceitful nature of their message.

The six published books are:

Harry Potter and the Sorcerer's Stone

Harry Potter and the Chamber of Secrets

Harry Potter and the Prisoner of Azkaban

Harry Potter and the Goblet of Fire

Harry Potter and the Order of the Phoenix

Harry Potter and the Half Blood Prince

It is extremely common for Harry Potter books to be read to students during class time in schools in spite of the fact that the Potter series favors morally flawed, egocentric characters who lie and somehow justify it, practice occult techniques, use profanity and frequently depict violence. In some schools teachers decorate their classrooms to look like various locations in Harry's world. Others have designed learning experiences based on the books and even encouraged students to create Harry Potter games and activities. Major publishers have released study books and classroom discussion guides designed to help teachers lead students through "the origins and mysteries of Harry's world"[1] including the occult themes.

Nearly every facet of occultism is thinly disguised in the series including alchemy, astrology, spells, mediumship, and other occultic practices. There are untold numbers of books written on witchcraft and the occult but none more ingeniously packaged to attract children like this one.

---

[1] Beacham's Sourcebook: Exploring Harry Potter, Beacham Publishing, Osprey FL, Section VI

The Harry Potter books desensitize both children and adults to the forbidden and dangerous world of pagan occult magic spoken of in the Scriptures. And let us not forget the Scriptures remind us that we are in spiritual warfare and that Christians should have nothing to do with such practices.

As we consider the dangers of Harry Potter, we need to remember the warning of Jesus when He said in Matthew 18:5,6, *and whoever welcomes a little child like this in my name welcomes me. But if anyone causes one of these little ones who believe in me to sin, it would be better for him to have a large millstone hung around his neck and to be drowned in the depths of the sea.*

Is it possible that the real Harry Potter is an evil spirit? The author, J.K. Rowling stated that in 1990 as she was traveling on a train, without any warning, she suddenly saw Harry *"very, very clearly"* in her mind. He came into her thoughts out of nowhere as a *"fully formed individual...Harry just strolled into my head...I really did feel he was someone who walked up and introduced himself in my mind's eye. I have no idea why he chose to come to me."*[2]

Many who try to justify their children reading the books say that is just fantasy and there is no really occultism to the books. However, Ms. Rowling admits that approximately one-third of what she has written is based on actual occultism. Some scenes are not only based on reality, but often are also described using details taken verbatim from sorcery and witchcraft.[3]

In the Harry Potter series, the years of training at Hogwart's School parallel the magical training in real life Ophidian Witchcraft which has to do with serpent veneration. In Ophidian Witchcraft ancient Runes are studied. In Prisoner of Azkaban, page 57 we read "Those are my books...Divination, the study of ancient Runes."[4] Those involved in Ophidian Witchcraft study divination. In Prisoner of Azkaban, p. 103 we read "We will be covering the basic methods of Divination this year." Ophidian Witchcraft teaches spellcasting. In Sorcerer's Stone, p. 66 we read "All students shall have a copy of each of the following: The Standard Book of Spells." Werewolf and animal transformation is taught in Ophidian Witchcraft. In the Sorcerer's Stone, p. 134 we read "Transformation is some of the most complex and dangerous magic you will ever learn at Hogwarts. And in Prisoner of Azkaban, p. 353 we read "It is very painful to turn into a werewolf...(my friends) could each turn into a different animal." Then Ophidian Witchcraft teaches the magical lore and the history

---

[2] Quoted in Reuter's *"Harry Potter strolled into My Mind,"* July 17, 2000. Interview on the Diane Rehm Show, WAMU, National Public Radio, October 20, 1999.

[3] J.K. Rowling, interview on The Diane Rehm Show, WAMU, National Public Radio, October 20, 1999

[4] Ancient Runes is one of the many classes of study in Book III. Runes are ancient Germanic characters used for writing things that one does not want others to be able to read. Runes can also be used for magickal writings and forms of divination.

of magic. In Sorcerer's Stone, p. 263 we read "Their very last exam was History of Magic.

The Harry Potter fantasy also points the reader to books in real occultism. For instance in Harry Potter book 1, page 66 and book 3, page 43 there is reference to The Standard Book of Spells. In real occultism there is a Book of Spells written in 1997 by Arthur Edward Waite. In Harry Pottter book 1, page 66 and book 3, page 5 there is reference to A History of Magic. In real occultism Eliphas Levi wrote The History of Magic in 1997. In Harry Potter book 1, page 66 there is reference to One Thousand Magical Herbs. In real occultism Scott Cunningham wrote Encyclopedia of Magical Herbs in 1985. And finally, in Harry Potter book 1, page 66 there is a reference to Magical Drafts & Potions. In real occultism Magick Potions: How to Prepare was written in 1998 by Gurina Dunwich.

What about the fictional characters in the Harry Potter series? Do they have any occult significance? Indeed they do. The following characters in the series have real world occultic counterparts.

Adalbert – in reality was a French mystic who claimed he could fortell the future and read thoughts.

Vablatsky – in reality this is probably an anagram for Blavatsky who lived from 1831 to 1891 and was the founder of Theosophy[5]. He also helped spread the concepts of Buddhism and reincarnation in America.

Minerva McGonagall – was one of Harry's teachers. In reality the name refers to the Roman goddess of agriculture, navigation, spinning, weaving and needlework.

Argus Filch – was Hogwart's caretaker. In reality the name refers to the Greek mythological giant with a hundred eyes.

Circe – in reality was a witch from Homer's *The Iliad* who could transform men into animals.

Draco Malfoy – in reality refers to astrology. Draco means dragon. The dragon is usually associated with guardians of temples and treasures.

Morgana & Merlin – in reality these names are taken from the King Authur legends. Merlin is Arthur's wizard mentor and Morgana is said to be heavily based on "Morrighan" an ancient Celtic goddess.

Cliodna – in reality is a Druid/ Celtic goddess who is still worshipped

---

[5] Theosophy is an occult blending of metaphysical thought, spiritualism, channeling, science, eastern philosophy, transcendentalism, and mental healing.

today by contemporary pagans and witches and is Ireland's pagan goddess of beauty.

Bane & Firenze –Finally *Harry Potter and the Sorcerer's Stone* plainly introduces astrology through the words of these two Centaurs. In reality a Centaur is a mythological beast with the torso and head of a man and hindquarters of a horse.

Rowling has many references in the Harry Potter series to various demonic entities deeply connected to magic, witchcraft, and sorcery.

Occult practices are numerous and frequent in the Harry Potter series. Following is a partial list of occult practices found in the series.

Fortune Telling – plays a prominent role in *Prisoner of Azkaban*

Magical Potions – are made from various herbs and fungi and play an extremely important role in Harry's education beginning early in *Sorcerer's Stone* (Book I)

Ancient Runes – one of the many classes of study in Book III. Runes are ancient Germanic characters used for writing things which one does not want others to be able to read. Runes can also be used for magical workings and forms of divination.

Arithmancy – a form of divination studied in Book III. It dates all the way back to the ancient Greeks and Chaldeans and is used as a means of discerning the winner of a battle.

Numerology – a form of divination studied in Book III. It analyzes the symbolism of numbers and ascribes numerical values to the letters of the alphabet.

Palmistry – a pseudoscience based on the lines and markings of a person's palm supposedly used to reveal a person's future.

Tea Leaves – the pattern of leaves is interpreted by swirling the dregs of a teacup three times and then dumping it on a saucer.

Fire Omens – read as an occultist gazes at the movement of flames while throwing leaves, twigs or incense into the fire. The changes in coloring and intensity of the flames are then interpreted as omens of things to come.

Charms – throughout the Potter books the characters are either studying or working "charms." A charm is an incantation of some kind designed to bring about a positive effect. The incantations can also be used to endow any object (amulet or talisman) with magical power.

These practices are clearly forbidden in God's Holy Word.

With book four in the series there is an increase in murder and torture. Muggle[6] killings are "done for fun" by Vordemort's followers (p. 143). There is the killing of two wizards (p. 531), the killing of another death eater (p. 589), the torture of countless Muggles (p. 589), a good wizard and his witch wife being tortured to the point of insanity (pp. 595, 603), Cedric's murder in front of Harry (p. 638), Pettigrew severing off his own hand to put in a boiling cauldron (pp. 641-642), Harry having blood drained into a vial after being slashed in the arm by Pettigrew (p. 642), Voldemort's statement that his survival depends on drinking a mixture of snake venom and unicorn blood (p. 656), and a child killing his father and turning the body into a bone and burying it (p. 690).

Profanity becomes more prevalent in book four. Following are a few examples: "Damn" (p. 43), "No one at the bank gives a damn how I dress" (p. 63), "Damn them" (p. 127), "Yeah, give Ron a good kick up the ass" (p. 290), "I don't give a damn" (p. 470), "He damn near beat it" (p. 232), "You're a damn good flier" (p. 344), "Damn leg" (p. 561), "What the hell do you think your doing?" (p. 626)

Author J.K.Rowling has stated that her young characters will be "discovering their hormones" as they grow up. In book four, *Goblet of Fire,* hints of sexuality are beginning to appear and remember there are still three more books to be published. In *Goblet of Fire* p. 84, an elderly wizard complains about having to trade his loose-fitting robe in for pants, saying: "I'm not putting them on...I like a healthy breeze 'round my privates, thanks. Later in book four on page 103 during the Quidditch World Cup, the Bulgarian mascots are about one hundred veelas – i.e., extremely sensual, highly erotic attractive pseudo-human females. They are "the most beautiful women Harry had ever seen." Finally on pages 252-253 we are told their intensely erotic movements cause wild, half-formed thoughts to race through Harry's dazed mind. Ron meets a half-Veelas and instantly falls in puppy-LUST.

The morals presented in the Potter books are anti-God and anti-Christian. The books are definitely drawing our children towards witchcraft. "Who wouldn't choose a wizard's life?" asked TIME magazine.[7] Even authentic, real Wiccans are "charmed" by the Potter series, according to the Associated Press.[8] Anything that true witches find good and charming certainly ought to be viewed with suspicion by any serious Christian.

---

[6] In *Harry Potter and the Sorcerer's Stone*, pg. 55 we read that Muggles are humans with no magical abilities whatsoever, totally "non-magic folk." Author J. K. Rowling consistently portrays Muggles as a narrow minded callous group of persons unable to grasp the glory of magic (*Sorcerer's Stone* – pp. 2,3,4,22). They are incredibly slow when it comes to perceiving truth, although as one witch put it in *Sorcerer's Stone* – pg. 10 "They're not completely stupid." Children reading the series soon conclude parents and grandparents are Muggles.

[7] TIME, 9/20/1999

[8] "Potter Charms Modern-Day Witches" by Deepti Hajela, AP 1/30/2000

The Harry Potter books are filled with explicit evil, disgusting witchcraft. Following is just an example. Imagine your child reading about:

The animal sacrifice of a cat[9]

Blood sacrifices[10]

Cutting off the hand of a living person for a ritual[11]

Boiling what seems to be a baby or fetus alive in a cauldron[12]

Possible demon possession[13]

Werewolves[14] & vampires[15]

Bringing an evil wizard back from the dead through the shedding of blood[16]

Astral projection or soul travel[17]

Casting spells and levitation[18]

Animal transformation[19]

Being taught people can exist without their souls[20]

Harry takes mood-altering drugs (which are actually real herbs that are used by witches and   shamans[21]

Use of the "Hand of Glory," a grisly occult artifact that is the severed hand of

---

[9] Harry Potter and the Chamber of Secrets, p. 139.

[10] Harry Potter and the Philosopher's Stone, p. 656

[11] Ibid. p. 641

[12] Goblet of Fire, p. 666. A careful reading of this passage reveals that the fetus-like character which is thrown into the cauldron is actually Lord Voldemort. However, many will not get this point and it is still very disturbing.

[13] Goblet of Fire, p. 653-54.

[14] Harry Potter and the Prisoner of Azkaban pp. 345, 381

[15] Ibid., p. 147

[16] Harry Potter and the Goblet of Fire, p. 463

[17] Ibid., pp. 667-669

[18] Ibid., pp. 344-45

[19] Ibid. p. 534

[20] Harry Potter and the Prisoner of Azkaban p. 247

[21] Harry Potter and the Sorcerer's Stone, p. 137, 286-87

a hanged murderer. Its fingers are lit and burned as candles. The hand is placed in a house to make everyone in the house fall into a spell[22].

Belief that death is just the "next great adventure." Although a true statement for Christians, for non-Christians like Harry, death is a one way ticket to hell.[23]

Moving through the books it becomes obvious that Harry, the young wizard, encounters ever increasing darkness. Liesl Schillinger, in her assessment of Harry Potter and the Half-Blood Prince for the *New York*

Times Book review said the latest book is filled with "secrets, deepening bonds, betrayals and brutal lessons, many of them coming from the sinister Harry-hating Severus Snape, master of the dark arts," which make this book "far darker than those that preceded" it. "Suffice it to say that this new volume culminates in a finish so scorchingly distressing that the reader closes the book quaking, knowing that out of these ashes, somehow, the phoenix of [author J.K.] Rowling's fiction will rise again – but worrying about how on earth Harry will cope until it does," Schillinger wrote.[24]

In another *Times* review, Michiko Kakutani noted that Harry sees the death of another important figure in his life in the latest book, Harry Potter and the Half-Blood Prince, which she calls "the darkest and most unsettling installment yet." Kakutani said Harry feels increasingly isolated. "The terrible things that Ms. Rowlings describes as being abroad in the green and pleasant land of England, reads like a grim echo of events in our own post 9/11, post 7/7 world..." Kakutani wrote.[25]

In Deuteronomy 18:10-12 God instructs us to *let no one be found among you who sacrifices his son or daughter in the fire, who practices divination or sorcery, interprets omens, engages in witchcraft, or casts spells, or who is a medium or spiritist or who consults with the dead. Anyone who does these things is detestable to the Lord...* Concerning vengeance in the Harry Potter books God says in Leviticus 19:18 *Do not seek vengeance...Love your neighbor as yourself."* And in Romans 12:17-18,21 God says *Do not repay anyone evil for evil...if it is possible, as far as it depends on you...Do not be overcome with evil, but overcome evil with good.* God stands opposed to the contents of the Harry Potter books and we need to guide our children accordingly. We are instructed to overcome evil with good.

---

[22] Harry Potter and the Prisoner of Azkaban p. 52

[23] Harry Potter and the Sorcerer's Stone, p. 302

[24] New York Times, July 31, 2005

[25] New York Times, July 16, 2005

Appendix F

Magic the Gathering
(card game)

Is *Magic: The Gathering* a card game or a series of collectable cards? The cover of the Revised Edition rule book calls it "A Fantasy Trading Card Game."[26] In reality it is a carefully crafted, well-marketed game where every card is collectable. There are five major editions to the game with over 1800 separate cards in existence. The games popularity has grown rapidly since the first edition was released in 1993.

Magic: The Gathering is unlike series of collector cards in that *Magic* cards can be used to play a card game which is different every time it is played. More than a card game, it is a game played in the minds of the players, a game of the imagination.

Each player (generally two) takes the role of the wizard of Dominia, a being that wanders the multiple planes and dimensions of existence in search of power. When two wizards clash, they duel it out by drawing upon their five sources (or *colors*) of magic power (*mana*) to conjure *creatures* to fight against their foe. They also cast spells on themselves (which are usually helpful) and against their foes or their foe's *creatures, lands and artifacts.* Finally they will employ artifacts, i.e. a "magically powered object," to channel magical energy for their use.[27] The duel continues until one wizard is dead.

All *Magic* cards come in one of two types: *land* cards and *spell* cards. The spell cards can be further divided into three subtypes: spells which summon creatures, spells which directly affect creatures and environments, and spells which conjure up artifacts. Both the land and spell cards are used in combat. The land cards provide a source of power or mana and the spell cards "do the work." Combat is carried out by laying down one or more of these four basic categories of cards. Each of these categories of cards work to attack the opposing wizard or his creatures, support or heal the attacking wizard or his creatures, or change the environment of the game. Each card's type and specifics are listed on the front of the card.

---

[26]Garfield, Richard. "Magic: The Gathering, A Fantasy Trading Card Game (Rulebook)." Wizards of the Coast, Inc., Renton, WA 98057-0707, 1994.

[27]Garfield, Richard. "The Magic: The Gathering Pocket Players' Guide." Wizards of the Coast, Inc., Renton, WA 98057-0707, 1994.

The content of this game is the key for deciding whether it is good or bad, helpful or harmful. The content of *Magic* can be most easily examined by breaking down the hundreds of cards and other information into categories. Most *Magic* cards can be put into one of the following categories: Combat and Violence, Magic Spells, The Real Occult, Life and Death, Spiritism, Necromancy and Divination, and Sacrifice.

What Has the Bible to Say

Combat & Violence - The Bible says much about unjust combat and gratuitous violence. Read Exodus 20:13; Hosea 4:1-2; Matthew 26:51-52; Luke 6:27-28.

Magic Spells - The Bible never condones the use of magic spells and calls those who do such things an "abomination." The Bible does not make light of magic nor does it deny it's existence. It affirms the reality not fantasy of magic in the world and condemns every use of it. Deuteronomy 18:10-14; Isaiah 47:9b, 15b; Leviticus 19:26; Micah 5:12,15; Malachi 3:5.

The Real Occult - This game contains real occult symbols such as: Anch, Palmistry, Circle of Protection, Pentacle, Goat's Head and the Magic Circle. Why does it contain real occult symbols? To make the game more real? To desensitize or familiarize players with them? A good summary of the overall message of the Bible regarding occult practices is God's word to the people of Israel as they were about to enter the land of Canaan in Deuteronomy 18:9-14.

Life and Death - The cards indicate two fundamental principles of the game: 1) death is not permanent, and 2) actions are not permanent. The consequences of an action can almost always be undone by the proper spell. The Bible, on the other hand, explicitly states that death is a one-time experience, followed by some type of judgment, and people are ultimately responsible for their actions. See Hebrews 9:27; Psalms 89:48; Ecclesiastes 3:1-2; Psalms 39:4; 1 Corinthians 15:25-26; and Genesis 3:19.

Spiritism, Necromancy and Divination - There are several other specific occult practices which are seen in *Magic*. Some are mentioned in passing, while others are the focus of a given card. On any card, two or more practices may overlap as well since some of the practices are quite broad. [Spiritism is used in both the broad and the specific senses within the game. In the broad sense, all of the "Summon Creature" type cards are a form of Spiritism. In the specific sense, several cards focus on summoning spirits for information or service.] Listed below are some of these practices with definitions.

> **Divination** - the act of divining; sorcery; soothsaying; pagan contrast to true prophecy or prophesying; man's attempt to know and control the world and future **apart** from the true God using

means other than human; foretelling or foreseeing the future or discovering hidden knowledge through reading omens, dreams, using lots, astrology, or necromancy.[28]

Spiritism - Worship of or communication with the supposed spirits of the dead. The Bible seems to indicate that these spirits are demons in disguise.[29]

Shaman - A medicine man or witch doctor.[30]

Necromancy - A practice in which the "spirits of the dead" are summoned to provide omens relating to future events or to discover secrets of the past.[31]

Zombies - In Vodoum, a reanimated corpse whose soul has been possessed by another through magic...Actually, a trick combining drugs and hypnosis.[32]

Again the Bible is very clear on God's condemnation of such practices. See Deuteronomy 18:10-14; Leviticus 19:31; 1 Chronicles 10:13.

Sacrifice - According to the rules of *Magic,* a sacrifice is "a cost that can not be prevented."[33] In the context of playing a game, this is the killing of a summoned being (human, demi-human, animal) to gain power or advantage. The target has to be someone the player controls and has decided to kill in this way. In no other games is there as much sacrificing as in *Magic.* In the game, the sacrificing is taken in quite a light-hearted manner with sacrificing explained as just one more strategy used to win. Compare this to the Bible's view of sacrificing in Leviticus 18:21; Jeremiah 32:35; and Deuteronomy 18:9-10a.

---

[28]Arthur, Kay. "Lord is it Warfare? Teach Me to Stand," Multnomah Press, Portland, OR 97220, 1991.

[29]Amstutz, Wendell. "Exposing and Confronting Satan & Associates," National Counseling Resource Center, Rochester, MN, 1991.

[30]Ibid

[31]Ibid

[32]Ibid

[33]Garfield, Richard. "The Magic: The Gathering Pocket Players' Guide," Wizards of the Coast, Inc., Renton, WA 98057-0707, 1994

Appendix G

Satanic Ritual Calendar

January

1   New Years Day

      Druid feast day, no sacrifice

7   St. Winebald Day

      Blood, animal/human sacrifice (dismemberment) of male 15-33 if human

17 Satanic Revels

      Sexual, oral, anal, vaginal of female age 7-17

20-27   Abduction, ceremonial preparation and holding of Sacrificial victim for Candlemas

      Sexual and blood. Oral, anal, vaginal, human sacrifice of a female or child, any age

29 St. Agnes Eve.

      Casting of spells

February

2   Candlemas (Sabbat Festival) Satan Revels St. Walpurgis Day

      Blood/sexual, animal or human, female 7-17

25 St. Walpurgis Day

      Blood, communion of blood and dismemberment of animal

March

1   St. Eichatadt

      Drinking of human blood for strength and homage to the demons, any age, male or female

20 var. Spring Equinox

> Orgies, oral, anal, vaginal, any age, male or female

Shrovetide

> 3 days before Ash Wednesday – a Witch Sabbat

April

17 var. Day of Christ's Crucifixion

> Blood, human sacrifice (may be a crucifixion), male only (adult)

18var. Easter Eve Day

> Blood, human sacrifice, male or female (adult)

21-26   Abduction ceremonial preparation and holding of sacrificial victim for Grand climax

> None

24 St. Mark's Eve

> Divining and herb gathering

26-May 1 Grand Climax

> Da Meur, Corpus De Baahl, female 1-25

30   Walpurgisnacht Roodmas Day/Beltane Eve. Often celebrated with a festival that includes bonfires and fertility rites. Greatest Witches Sabbat

> Blood, human and/or animal (a Celtic/Druid holiday, time for planting crops. Any age.

May

1   Beltane, Walpurgis Day, May Day

> Druid fire festival, coven initiations

June

21 Feast Day

> Orgies, oral, anal, vaginal, animal and/or human sacrifice, any age, male or female or animal

July

1   Demon Revels

     Blood, druids sexual association with demons, any age, female

25   St. James Day

     Gathering of herbs

August

1   Lammas Day (Sabbat Festival, Feast of Son god. Harvest season begins

     Blood, animal and/or human, any age, male or female

3   Satanic Revels

     Sexual, oral, anal, vaginal, female 7-17

24   St. Bartholomew's Day

     Great SAbbat, Fire Festival, large herb gathering

September

7   Marriage to the Beast (Satanic marriages occur)

     Sexual, sacrifice/dismemberment, female infant to 21

20   Midnight Host

     Blood, dismemberment (hands planted) female infant to age 21

22   Feast Day (Fall Equinox)

     Orgies, oral, anal, vaginal, any age, male, female, or animal

October

13   Halloween backward (31 inverted to 13)

     Preparation for All Hallows Eve, Samhain (Halloween)

28-30   Satanist High (Holy day related to Halloween)

     Human sacrifice each day, any age, male or female

29-Nov. 1   All Hallows Eve (Halloween)

     Blood, sexual climax associated with the demons, any age, male or female

November

4   Satanic Revels

        Sexual, oral, anal, vaginal, female 7-17

December

22   Feast Day (Sabbat Festival)

        Orgies, oral, anal, vaginal, any age, male or female or animal

23   Demon Revels

        DaMeur, High Grand Climax, any age, male or female, animal or human

24   Christmas Eve

        Blood, receive body parts as Christmas presents, infant male, (mocking of the baby Jesus)

Appendix H

Wicca

Wicca is an occult religion based on witchcraft. And although witchcraft can be traced back several centuries before the coming of Christ, for the purpose of this information, we will concentrate on Wicca's modern revival in 1949.[34]

As the basic functional unit is a coven (except in the case of a solitary), Wiccans pool their financial resources in order to purchase that which is necessary for the running of the coven such as robes, cakes, wine, etc.

Gerald B. Gardner is generally credited with the modern revival of Wicca in England in the 1950's, although he was neither the first to practice nor the founder of Witchcraft. In 1949 Gardner published his *High Magic's Aid*, a novel about "The Craft" under the pen name of "Scire,"[35] which was later followed by several others.

Throughout his life, Gardner was fascinated with many different aspects of the Occult. He had been a follower in varying degrees of such people and philosophies as Aleister Crowley, Ordo Templi Orientis, the Hermetic Order of the Golden Dawn and Rosicrucianism.[36]

The Craft and The Old Religion are sometimes used to refer to the magical aspects of Wicca or to its revival of ancient non-Christian traditions. Historians have credited Doreen Valiente, a follower of Gardner who he initiated into the Craft in 1953, with "increasing the emphasis on the Goddess[37]

While followers of Witchcraft had been in the United States since it's inception, Witchcraft's greatest growth took place during the 1960's and 1970's, during a general revival of interest in the Occult.[38] Historians of Wicca generally credit Raymond and Rosemary Buckland with Wicca's successful spread into American society. The came to the U.S. in 1962, having been followers of Gardner.[39]

---

[34] **The Encyclopedia of Witches and Witchcraft**, Rosemary Ellen Guiley, pp. 368-374.

[35] **Drawing Down the Moon**, Margot Adler, p. 61

[36] **The Encyclopedia of Witches and Witchcraft,** Rosemary Ellen Guiley, p. 375

[37] Ibid

[38] Ibid

[39] **Encyclopedia of Occultism and Parapsychology**, Leslie Shepard, Vol. 1, p. 133

In 1973, one of the most prolific publishers of Occult material, Llewellyn Press, *"sponsored a meeting of Witches in Minneapolis."* This gathering was attended by Witches from seventy-three different Craft traditions and attempted to write a statement of principles. The attempt failed to satisfy all participants and was followed in 1974 by the Council of American Witches which did finally complete the Principles of Wiccan Belief. Later, in 1975, thirteen covens would *"ratify the Covenant of the Goddess."*[40]

Most modern followers prefer the term Wicca to Witchcraft. *"As a religion Witchcraft often is called 'Wicca," an Old English term for 'witch,' in order to counter the negative stereotype of Witches as ugly, evil, and Devil-worshippers"*[41]

Because of the autonomous nature of Wicca, several key groups, known as traditions, have sprung into existence over the past few decades. Some of these prominent traditions include the Gardnerian tradition which originated in England, by Gerald Gardner in the 1950's and is one of the most modern Wiccan traditions; the Alexandrian tradition which originated in England in the 1960's by Alexander Sanders and whose rituals are said to be modified Gardenarian; the Dianic tradition which is the WitchCult in Western Europe, has been pegged as the "feminist" movement of the Craft, focuses mainly on the goddess, and is tracked back to Margaret Murray in 1921; the Celtic Wicca which is a mix using Celtic/Druidic pantheon, stressing on the elements (earth, air, fire, water) and the ancient ones; and finally the Seax-Wica tradition founded in 1973 by Raymond Buckland, who authored this tradition without breaking his original Gardnerian oath.[42]

---

[40] **Drawing Down the Moon**, pp. 99-103

[41] **Harper's Encyclopedia of Mystical and Paranormal Experience**, p. 647

[42] **Encyclopedia of Witches and Witchcraft**, pp. 377-379

Basic Beliefs

Wicca is a nature-based belief system. The natural world (i.e. trees, grass, rocks, mountains, etc.) is seen as a part of God. Christianity, on the other hand, teaches that these things were created by God, and not to be worshipped.

Wiccans believe in a dual male/female divinity. The god and goddess are seen as separate but equal deities, each with unique talents and virtues. Some traditions see all of the gods and goddesses of the world as "faces" of the two true deities. Others worship a god and goddess whose nature changes with the seasons.

They believe that the natural world, the creatures of the world (including humans) and the divine are inseparable. Harm done to any of the aspects reflects on the others, causing pain and suffering needlessly in the spiritual and physical realms. As a result, many Wiccans are ardent environmentalists.

One other group that is Wiccan in its overall philosophy is the School of Wicca founded by Gavin and Yvonne Frost. By some estimates this group *"may have created a hundred covens through its activities"*.[43]

---

[43] **Drawing Down the Moon**, p. 125

Organizational Structure

Each individual coven is autonomous and therefore have their own organizational structure. Generally the high priestess is considered the leader of the Coven.

Doctrine

The theology of Wicca varies from tradition to tradition and even more from coven to coven. The following are a few of the doctrines that most Wiccan covens will believe and practice.

1. Autonomy. *"There is no central authority or liturgy; various traditions have their own rituals, philosophy and beliefs, Some have added elements from Eastern, Native American Indian, aboriginal and shamanic systems; others have injected politics into their traditions. New ritual, songs, chants, and poetry are continually created."*[44]

2. Experience vs. Dogma. Because of the autonomy of each Coven and even to a large degree of each individual member of Wicca, the experience of the individual is of greater importance than any set of dogmatic doctrines. *"Generally speaking Witches are very open-minded people, especially where religion is concerned. They have no hard and fast 'Commandments,' no catechisms".*[45] Adler adds, *"By creating our own divinities we create mental steps for ourselves, up which we can mount toward realizing ourselves as divine. The lack of dogma in the Craft, the fact that one can worship the goddess without believing in her, that one can accept the goddess as 'Muse' and the Craft as a form of ancient knowledge to be tested by experience; these are precisely the things that have caused the Craft to survive, to revive, and to be re-created in this century."*[46]

3. Rituals. The individual or Coven experiences are gained through self-designed rituals. *"We are talking about the rituals that people create to get in touch with those powerful parts of themselves that cannot be experienced on a verbal level. Rituals are also created to acknowledge on this deeper level the movement of the seasons and the natural world, and to celebrate life and its processes."*[47]

---

[44] **Encyclopedia of Witches and Witchcraft,** p. 376

[45] ibid

[46] **Drawing Down the Moon,** p. 173

[47] **Drawing Down the Moon,** pp. 197-198

They celebrate 8 Sabbats (seasonal festivals) in the year, four Greater and four Lesser. The Greater Sabbats include Imbolc, Beltane, Lughnasa and Samhain while the Lesser Sabbats comprise the Summer and Winter Solstices and the Spring and Autumn Equinoxes. In addition 13 Esbats are convened each lunar month (every 28 days), usually around the time of the full moon, for the purpose of conducting coven ritual/s and business. Additional rituals include the conferring of the three degrees of Wicca, Wiccanings (the blessing of a new-born child), Handfastings (the marrying of a couple for 1 year and 1 day) and Requiems (celebrations for the dead).[48]

Wiccan rituals may also include the performance of simple candle-burning (usually but not always practiced by an individual witch) and workings such as the "Drawing Down of the Moon" during which the coven High Priest/ess invokes the goddess. Cord magic rituals may also be performed and along with candle-burning may be classed as spell-casting. New rituals and new ways of performing old rituals are continually being devised. The number of rituals and their nature is limited only by the imagination of the Wiccan.

4. Magic: Many of the rituals involve divination or magic. *"In his book of shadows, Gardner lists eight ways to raise magical power (singly or in combination): (1) meditation or concentration; (2) chants, spells, and invocations; (3) trance and astral projection; (4) incense, wine and drugs; (5) dancing; (6) blood control by binding parts of the body with cords; (7) scourging (not enough to draw blood); (8) ritual sex."*[49]

5. Ethics? The Wiccan Rede perhaps best describes the Wiccan ethic in one sentence: *"An it harm none (if it harms noone) do what you will."*[50] Sometimes witches perform "black" magick on certain individuals or groups. Two famous British Wiccans, Janet and Stewart Farrar try to justify such actions with the comment that *"...if somebody is known to be evil acting and harming others, witches are fully justified in stopping him."*[51] One more recent addition is a strong feminist ethic which has given it political overtones as well illustrated in the newspaper article which states: *"...Women want to be active in their spirituality, not simply the receivers of someone else's – usually a man's-expression of spirituality..."*[52]

---

[48] **Farrar and Farrar,** 1984

[49] **Harper's Encyclopedia of Paranormal Experience,** p. 649

[50] **Farrar and Farrar,** 1984

[51] Ibid, p. 141

[52] **Rowe and Cavender,** 1991, p. 266

6. The Rule of Three: The Rule of Three states: *"Any energy that you send out will return to you three-fold."* This includes magical energy, as well as emotional and spiritual energy. Wiccans interpret this rule to mean that any good works, bad works, arguments, etc. will return to them three times as powerfully as they left.

7. Goddess Worship: Worship of the goddess sometimes manifests itself as the worship of *"the Mother Goddess in her three aspects of Maiden, Mother, and Crone."* Sometimes it is the worship of *"what we potentially are."*[53] In many covens the high priestess is seen as the personification of the *"mother goddess who is the principal deity of witchlore."*[54]

8. Feminism: Even though not all feminists are Wiccans, many find the philosophy of Wicca compatable. *"Women who have come to the goddess outside the channels of Neo-Paganism and the Craft are beginning to find rituals and concepts that allow for the same idea. They are finding the goddess within themselves and within all women. And, as might be expected, those feminists who have found joy in rituals, and who have discovered that the concept of 'goddess' feels right inside, are often drawn into the Craft."*[55]

9. Evil: Wiccan groups do not accept the existence of evil. They explain: *"Wicca can be defined as a pagan mystery religion with a polarized deity and no personification of evil."* In the Principles of Wiccan Beliefs is stated, *"We do not accept the concept of 'absolute evil' nor do we worship any entity known as 'Satan' or 'The Devil' as defined by the Christian tradition."*[56]

10. The Horned God: Some Wiccan covens not only worship a mother goddess, but also a masculine deity. *"Many Craft traditions worship a god, related to the ancient horned lord of animals, the god of the hunt, the god of death and lord of the forests."*[57]

11. Seasonal Festivals: The worship of nature or natural order is of paramount importance. *"Wicca is basically a fertility cult and its great festivals are geared to the seasons."*[58]

---

[53] **Drawing Down the Moon**, pp. 10-11, 202

[54] **Man, Myth and Magic**, Vol 14, p. 1866

[55] **Drawing Down the Moon**, p. 205

[56] Ibid, pp. 100, 103

[57] Ibid, p. 11

[58] **Man, Myth and Magic**, Vol. 14, p.1866

Key dates on the Wiccan calendar correspond with some of the key dates on the Satanic calendar. For example:

Wicca – February 2 – Candlemas

Satanism – February 2 – Candlemas (Sabbat Festival), blood/sexual sacrifices, animal or human, female 7-17

Wicca – March 21 – spring equinox

Satanism – March 21 – spring equinox, orgies – oral, anal, vaginal, any age male or female

Wicca – April 30 – Beltane

Satanism - April 30 – Beltane, blood sacrifices – animal and/or human, any age

Wicca – June 22 – summer solstice

Satanism – June 21 – feast day, orgies – oral, anal, vaginal animal and/or human sacrifice, any age – male, female, or animal

Wicca – August 1 – August Eve

Satanism – August 1 – Lammas Day, animal and/or human blood sacrifices, any age male or female

Wicca – September 21 – autumn equinox

Satanism – September 20 – Midnight Host, blood sacrifice and dismemberment, hands planted, female infant to age 21

Wicca – October 31 – Halloween

Satanism – October 29 – November 1 – All Hallows Eve – blood and sexual sacrifice, sexual climax association with the demons, any age male or female

Wicca – December 21 – winter solstace

Satanism – December 22 – Feast Day (Sabbat Festival), orgies – oral, anal, vaginal, any age male or female or animal

What Does God Have to Say

Since followers of Wicca do not believe the Bible to be the Word of God, it is extremely difficult to show them the error of Wicca from a biblical point of view. However, from the Christian perspective, Wicca's teachings have been condemned for centuries.

1. Witchcraft and magic (enchantments) are condemned. Leviticus 19:26, 31; Deuteronomy 18:10-11; 2 Chronicles 33:6.
2. Worship of other gods (or of goddesses) is condemned. Exodus 20:3; 1 Kings 11:4-5.
3. Esteeming nature above God is condemned. Romans 1:21-25.
4. Satan and his influence of evil are real. Zechariah 3:2; Mathew 4:1-11; Luke 6:45.

And if time would permit a more detailed discussion these Scriptures are but the tip of the iceberg.

Beware Christians! Prospective members may be drawn from the public or from the friends and/or acquaintances of Wiccans if they are deemed suitable. A prime recruiting focus is on High School age individuals. Our children are being lured into Wicca. Late in 2001 we worked with a teen-age boy here in Florida who was a member of a Southern Baptist Church, attended youth meetings faithfully on Wednesday evenings, and professed Christ as Savior. However, he got involved in a local Wiccan Coven. He cast spells and was involved in astral projection among other occult practices. He had a curse placed upon him and this was causing much distress.

Unfortunately he was unwilling to renounce his activities within the coven, confess his sins, nullify the curse, and deal with the associated spirit activity. He is still suffering. Let's teach our youth to avoid such activities.

Appendix I

Hatha Yoga

The rising popularity of *Hatha-Yoga* in the Western world warrants a discussion of the practice of Yoga as a dangerous form of occultism.

Yoga is a system of physical exercises and mental discipline which is a vital part of Hindu religious philosophy aimed at the *union* of the human soul with the Universal Soul. The term *yoga* is from the Sanskrit meaning "union." This goal is supposed to be achieved through deep meditation and concentration, controlled breathing exercises, and certain physical postures. There are various types of yoga, each one a stage in the attainment of liberation from the cycle of reincarnation through union with the Universal Soul of God. The types of yoga are: Karma-yoga; Bhakti-yoga; Jnana-yoga; Raja-yoga, and Hatha-yoga already noted.

Raja-yoga constitutes what is generally thought of as yoga (in the West especially) and seems to have arisen about the second century B.C. Its origin is attributed to a Hindu sage named Patanjali. The primary source book for the system is entitled *Yogasutras.*

The final goal of yoga is deliverance from the endless cycle of rebirths (reincarnation) and the burden of Karma. The body is thought to be the prison of the soul, and man's bondage and adversity stem from this union of body and soul. Liberation of the soul from its prison comes through right knowledge of this fact. Through the yoga system of self-discipline and mental concentration the soul can be liberated from its bondage and will at death be absorbed by the Brahma or World Soul. Although for the present he is still in his body, he is able to rid himself of nature's control over him.

In Raja-yoga there are eight stages, the highest being *Samadhi*, which is the attainment of super-consciousness or trance. At this stage the yogin is said to achieve union with the Universal Soul and now has an awareness of true reality and knowledge. In this state the yogin may remain in a state of "hibernation," maintaining the same posture for weeks. Some have actually been buried for long periods while in this state of trance. Through yoga other occult powers of telepathy, clairvoyance, and astral projection of the soul are often achieved.

Along with the Eastern religions yoga has also penetrated the Western world. The most popular form of yoga most adapted to our Western culture is known as *Hatha-Yoga,* which is primarily a system of physical exercises and mental concentration concerned with health and longevity. However, yogis stress the fact that Hatha-yoga is not an end in itself, but preparation for the higher principles of Hindu philosophy. The unscriptural Hindu concept that the soul is imprisoned in the body and must be liberated is at the very center of Hatha-yoga. It is in direct conflict with the teaching of the Bible which asserts that the body is the Temple of the Holy Spirit and that the Christian is to glorify God in his body (1 Corinthians 6:19-20; cf. Romans 12:1-2).

In Hatha-yoga it is the *mind and soul* which are aimed at, according to one author and advocate of yoga. The physical exercises and mental disciplines are designed to overcome the body of flesh, for the *ultimate goal* is preparation of the soul for union with the Universal Soul. Whether or not one is aware of this purpose does not change the fact that in Hatha-yoga, like its other forms, *an individual is involving himself in Hinduism and opening himself to the influence and control of satanic forces.* There are instances of individuals becoming demonized by evil spirits through their practice of Hatha-yoga merely as a means of physical exercise.

There are thousands of classes in Hatha-yoga conducted daily all over America and Europe, not including those on television. Impressive numbers of these participants, moreover, are not involved in mere physical exercises, but are seeking self-knowledge, self-realization, and a spiritual experience through such occult meditation. A sincere approach to yoga ultimately leads into a study of Hindu philosophy, deep trance, the pagan chanting of Sanskirt phrases, and other mystical aspects of the occult. Participation in any form of the occult invariably results in some form of oppression by the powers of darkness which are operating behind the yoga system to ensnare the unwary.

Appendix J

How a Born-Again Believer Can Become Demonized

By: Rev. David Cotner
Missionary Church, Inc., Retired

The Question is Often Asked
"Can a Born-Again Believer be Demonized?"

Contrary to popular belief a born-again believer can be demonized. Most Christians today believe the "great myth" which is the belief that because I am a born-again believer, an evil spirit can not live in me because the Holy Spirit lives in me.

The word "*demonized*" comes from the Greek word "*daimonizomai*" which means "to have a demon." E.g. Mark 5:15-16. It is improper to say a person is possessed. The proper terminology is demonized. The result of demonization is control, not ownership, since Satan and evil spirits can own nothing.

There are two reasons for this: first of all they are created beings and not God the Creator and owner of everything (Psalm 24:1-2; 115:15-16; Ezekiel 28:13-15), and secondly, Christ has purchased us for God (Revelation 5:9).

The areas of control by the evil spirit are not in the person's spirit but in the person's soul (mind, emotions, will, and affections) occasionally resulting in physical manifestations.

Scripture references that teach about the trichotomy of the human nature (body, soul, and spirit) plus the warfare against the soul are: 1 Thessalonians 5:23; Hebrews 4:12; 1 Peter 2:11; Psalm 71:13; John 3:3-6; Romans 7:22-23; 8:10-16; 1 Corinthians 5:5; 6:17-20; Galatians 5:16-25.

The Biblical Evidence that a
Born-Again Believer can be Demonized

A DISCLAIMER

The Scriptures do not conclusively prove a born-again believer <u>can</u> be demonized. Neither do the Scriptures conclusively prove a born-again believer can <u>not</u> be demonized. However the Scriptures do conclusively prove that <u>people</u> can be demonized.

THE OLD TESTAMENT

1 Samuel 15:1-35 esp. 23; 16:14; 18:10

The demon was sent by God to torment Saul because of his disobedience to God (see also Matthew 18:34-35) and caused great changes in Saul's nature and controlled his physical behavior.

THE GOSPELS

Matthew 8:28-32 – Two violent men in the country of the Gadarenes.

Matthew 9:32-33 – The man who could not speak.

Mark 1:23-27 – The man in the Synagogue in Capernaum.

Luke 8:1-3 – Women who had been healed of evil spirits and followed Jesus.

Many other examples are found in the four Gospels

.THE BOOK OF ACTS

Acts 5:1-4 – The word "*filled*" in vs. 3 is the same word Paul uses in Ephesians 5:18 for a believer to "be filled or controlled with the Spirit." Satan and an evil spirit had taken control of Anannias' heart and produced the greed and lie.

THE EPISTLES

1 Corinthians 5:1,5 – This believer in the Corinthian church was living in an open, unrepentant incestuous relationship. Paul's only option was to turn the man over to Satan for discipline. He would be killed but at least his spirit would be saved.

1 Corinthians 10:14-22 – Paul clearly warns the believers not to "*share*" in demons. The word for "*share*" in Greek is the word "*fellowship*" or "*fellow participant.*"

Paul's point is that just as we have fellowship with Jesus during the eating of the bread and drinking of the cup during communion, so we have fellowship with demons during idol worship. Paul clearly states in vs. 21 that it is possible for a believer to "*drink the cup of demons*" and "*partake of the table of demons.*" This verse is not teaching about the Lord Jesus and a demon dwelling together in the believer at the same time, only that a believer can not have fellowship with the Lord Jesus at the same time he is having fellowship with a demon. Note also that unconfessed sin breaks our fellowship with God.

Ephesians 4:26-27 – Paul warns the Ephesian believers not to give the devil a "*place*" KJV, NIV is "*foothold*", NASB is "*opportunity.*" The common sense of the word in Greek is "*place*" or "*location.*" It can also have the transferred sense of "*opportunity.*" Unchecked anger gives the devil an opportunity to control a place in the believer's life.

1 Peter 5:8 – In Greek the word "*devour*" means "*drink down, swallow, digest.*" The Septuagint uses this word to translate the word "*swallow*" where the great fish "*swallowed*" Jonah.

Satan would like nothing better than to "*devour*" believers and destroy them. He does not have the power to do that, but he does have the power to control believer's lives to the point where their relationship with God is seriously hindered, they are in bondage to sin, and their lives are ineffective in service to Christ.

How Can an <u>Evil</u> Spirit Live in the
Same Body with the <u>Holy</u> Spirit?

TWO BIBLICAL ANSWERS

1. In the same way that the Holy Spirit can live in the same body with our sin and our sinful nature, (Romans 7:15-25) the Holy Spirit can live in the same body with a demon "squatter."

2. Our bodies are temples of the Holy Spirit. 1 Corinthians 3:16-17; 1 Corinthians 6:19-20; 2 Corinthians 6:16-18. The Old Testament temple was a "type" of the New Testament temple which is our body (John 2:19-20). In the Old Testament the temple could be defiled yet the presence of God was still there. 2 Kings 23:4-8).

The Experiential Evidence that a Born-Again
Believer can be Demonized

The experiences of many spiritual warfare counselors attest to this. One recommended book for reading would be Dr. Roger Boehm's – <u>In the Face of Evil, A Wake-Up Call for Christians</u> available through LuLu Publishing at lulu.com, or it can be ordered from your favorite bookstore.

C Fred Dickason – <u>Demon Possession & The Christian</u> p. 208-209

Neil T. Anderson – <u>The Bondage Breaker</u> p. 171-172

Timothy Warner – <u>Spiritual Warfare</u> p. 104-105

Mark I. Bubeck – <u>The Satanic Revival</u> (<u>The Rise of Fallen Angels</u>) p. 148

How can a Born-Again Believer
Become Demonized?

THROUGH PERSISTENT, UNREPENTANT SINNING Hebrews
12:1. Following are the major categories of sin which are known to be entry points for the control of evil spirits:

1. **All forms of lying** (John 8:44).   Includes deceiving and exaggerating as well as believing lies and deception.

2. **Unbelief** (Hebrews 3:12,19). Includes all doubting and lack of faith and trust in God and His Word.

3. **Pride** (Proverbs 16:18; 1 Peter 5:5).

4. **Anger** (Ephesians 4:26-27). Includes bitterness (Hebrews 12:15) and unforgiveness (Ephesians 4:31-32) which grows out of anger.

5. **Rebellion** (1 Samuel 15:23). Includes lack of submission to authority both in and outside the church (Hebrews 13:17; Romans 13:1-5).

6. **Sexual sins** (Romans 13:12-14; 1 Corinthians 6:9-20). Includes all forms of sexual activity outside of marriage.

7.

THROUGH CULT AND OCCULT INVOLVEMENT

All cults and occult activity is a satanic counterfeit of Christ, Biblical Christianity, the true works and ways of God and the Kingdom of God, 2 Corinthians 2:11; 11:14.

Brief List of Cults:

Hare Krishna, Scientology, Christian Science, Mormons, Unification Chuirch, The Way International, Bahai, Hinduism, Islam, Jehovah's Witnesses, Masonic Lodge, Theosophy.

Brief List of Occult Activity:

Ouija Board, Crystal Ball, Satanism, 8 Ball, Witchcraft, Séance, Palm Reading, Rod & Pendulum, Astrology, Telepathy, Satanic Ritual Abuse, Levitation, Light as a Feather & Stiff as a Board, Acupuncture, Magic or Lucky Charms, Blood Pacts, Dungeons & Dragons, Satanic Video Games, Psychic Hotline, Handwriting Analysis, Crystals, Tarot Cards, Black & White Magic, Wicca, Fortune Telling, Halloween & Related Activities, Spirit Guides, Astral Projection, Water Witching (divination) Wearing Magnets, Psychic Healings, ESP, Magic Cards & Game, Pokemon, Harry Potter, Magic Spells & Curses, Kabala, Native American Objects.

DEMONIC TRANSFERANCE

From your ancestors (Exodus 20:5-6; Lamentations 5:7) or from a demonized person through sexual activity outside the marriage bond or through sexual, physical, verbal, or emotional abuse (1 Corinthians 6:16).

SEEKING FOR SPIRITUAL GIFTS AND EMOTIONAL EXPERIENCES

Matthew 12:38-45; Acts 8:14-23; 1 Corinthians 12:1-3

Believers are most commonly demonized when they seek to speak in tongues, search for an emotional spiritual "high" and accept the indiscriminate laying on of hands. The proper way to "lay hands" on a person is by the elders of the church in obedience to James 5:14.

Speaking in tongues are very easy for a demon to counterfeit as are emotional "highs" 2 Corinthians 11:14. Laying on of hands is the prescribed means by which Satanists transfer power to each other.

It is always dangerous to seek for a gift or a spiritual experience that God may not wish to give you. In doing so you open yourself up to a demonic substitute. If you speak or pray in tongues be sure to test the spirit of the tongue, 1 John 4:1-2 (Any appropriate Biblical test questions may be used).

MISUSE OF BIBLE DOCTRINE

Ephesians 1:3; Colossians 2:9-10; 2 Timothy 3:16-17.

Examples:

In Ephesians 1:3 we are told that God has given to us every spiritual blessing in Christ, and in Colossians 2:9-10 we are told that we are complete in Christ. Therefore seeking for spiritual blessings and benefits outside of Christ Himself is dangerous. We may receive something, but it will not be from God.

Another example is when a believer is told to seek for the *baptism of the Spirit.*" The truth is that at the moment of salvation a person is baptized in the Spirit. I.e. the person is "placed into" the Spirit, the Spirit is "placed into" them, and they are "placed into" the church. (*To dip, submerge, or place into*" is the meaning of *'baptism"* in Greek). John 3:6-8; Romans 6:1-10; Galatians 3:26-28; 1 Corinthians 12:13. To seek the *"baptism of the Spirit"* after salvation is to open up one's-self to receiving a false & evil spirit.

Another example is when we pray for God to, "come and be with us" or we pray for, "more of Jesus" or, "more of the Holy Spirit." The truth is that Jesus is always with us (Hebrews 13:5) and God is omnipresent (Jeremiah 23:24). The truth is that when we receive Christ at the moment of salvation, God gives us all of Jesus and all of the Holy Spirit. However, they do not have all of us as far as their control of every area of our life. The process of being *"filled with the Spirit"* (Ephesians 5:18) is to allow Jesus through the Holy Spirit to *"fill"* (control) all of our life. Asking for "more" of God whom you already have in His fullness is dangerous for you are then open to receiving a demonic counterfeit. Asking God to "come" when He is already here is dangerous for you are then again open to receiving a false and evil spirit in your presence.

10 Signs of Possible Demonization
in the Born-Again Believer

1. Inability to gain victory over "besetting sins." Sexual sins, anger, rage, unforgiveness, resentment, unbelief, etc.
2. Inability to stop negative, abnormal and destructive behavior.
3. A persistent sense that, "Something is wrong but I don't know what. I've tried everything but I don't get any better."
4. A history of early childhood abuse or trauma.
5. A generational family history of identical problems.
6. Past or present involvements in cults, the occult, or sex outside of marriage.
7. Persistent unbelief and doubts over Biblical and spiritual issues.
8. A persistent problem concentrating during Bible reading, prayer, and worship services. Sometimes even being unable to read the Bible or memorize Scripture.
9. Chronic physical problems with no medical cause.
10. Paranormal or supernatural experiences. Such as hearing voices in your mind, seeing "shapes" in your room or house, hearing unexplainable sounds in the house, frequent nightmares, feeling an evil presence near you or touching you.

The Victory of the Born-Again Believer
Over Demonization

For the believer who is demonized victory is guaranteed.

Satan and his evil spirits have all been defeated by the Lord Jesus Christ through His death and resurrection. Genesis 3:15; 1 Corinthians 15:24-27; Colossians 1:15-23; 2:13-15; Hebrews 2:14-18; 1 Peter 3:22; 1 John 3:8; Revelation 19.11-16; 20:1-15.

The Believer is in complete victory over Satan and his hosts because we share in Christ's authority over them. Psalm 108:12-13; Matthew 12:28-29; 18:18; 28:18-20; Luke 10: 17-19; 2 Corinthians 10:4; Ephesians 1:17-2:6; Colossians 1:12-14; James 4:7; 1 John 4:4.

Highly recommended for every believer as a tool for spiritual growth, regardless of suspecting demonization, is Neil T. Anderson's "Seven Steps to Freedom in Christ." Each of the "7 Steps to Freedom" involves the four necessary elements for any believer to become free from bondage to evil spirits:

1. Examination for sin. 1 Corinthians 11:28
2. Confession of sin. 1 John 1:9
3. Repentance from sin. 2 Corinthians 7:8-10
4. Renouncing all evil spirits. James 4:7

When renouncing and evicting evil spirits from your life:

1. Identify the evil spirit and it's area of control ("place"). Ephesians 4:27
2. Remember your position & authority in Christ. Ephesians 1:17-2:6
3. Speak the name of the Lord Jesus Christ. Philippians 2:9-11
4. Speak the blood of the Lord Jesus Christ. Revelation 12:11
5. Speak the truth of the Word of God. John 8:32
6. Command the evil spirits, in the Name of the Lord Jesus Christ and by the power of His holy blood, to leave and go where the Lord Jesus Christ sends them, never to return.

In addition a highly successful way for a born-again believer to deal with demonization issues is by meeting with a qualified Christian counselor who uses the Christ-Centered Counseling method where the Lord Jesus Christ is the primary Counselor.

Bibliography

Bibliography

Anderson, Neil T., The Bondage Breaker, Eugene, OR, Harvest House, 1990.

Victory Over the Darkness, Ventura, CA, Regal, 1990.

Walking Through The Darkness, San Bernardino, CA., Here's Life Pub., 1991

The Seduction Of Our Children, Eigene, OR., Harvest House, 1991.

Released From Bondage, San Bernardino, CA., Here's Life Pub., 1991.

Living Free In Christ, Ventura, CA., Regal, 1993.

Setting Your Church Free, Ventura, CA., Regal, 1994.

Arnold, Clinton, 3 Crucial Questions about Spiritual Warfare, Grand Rapids, MI., Baker   Book House, 1997.

Barnhouse, Donald G., The Invisible War, Grand Rapids, MI, Zondervan, 1965.

Boehm, Roger, In the Face of Evil – A Wakeup Call for Christians, Titusville, FL, LuLu Publishing, 2006.

Bubeck, Mark, The Adversary, Chicago, IL., Moody Press, 1975.

Overcoming the Adversary, Chicago, IL, Moody Press, 1984.

The Rise Of Fallen Angels, Chicago, IL., Moody Press, 1995.

Raising Lambs Among Wolves, Chicago, IL., Moody Press, 1997.

Dickason, Fred, <u>Angels Elect & Evil</u>, Chicago, Illinois, Moody, 1975.

Demon Possession And The Christian, A New Perspective, Chicago, IL., Moody Press, 1987.

Friesen, James G. PhD, <u>Uncovering the Mystery of MPD</u>, San Bernardino, CA., Here's Life Publishers, Inc., 1992.

Gaeberlein, Arno C., <u>The Conflict of the Ages</u>, New York, N.Y., Publication Office "Our Hope," 1933.

Montgomery, J. Warwick, <u>Principalities and Powers</u>, Minneapolis, MN., Bethany Fellowship, 1975.

Russell, Jeffrey Burton, <u>Lucifer: The Devil in the Middle Ages</u>, Ithaca, NY, Cornell University Press, 1986.

Russell, Jeffrey Burton, <u>The Devil: Perceptions of Evil from Antiquity to Primitive Christianity, Ithaca</u>, NY, Cornell University Press, 1987.

Smith, Margaret, <u>Ritual Abuse</u>, San Francisco, CA., Harper, 1993.

Unger, Merrill F., <u>Biblical Demonology</u>, Chicago, IL., Scripture Press, 1955.

Wagner, Peter, <u>Wrestling With Dark Angels</u>, Ventura, CA., Regal Books, 1990.

<u>Engaging the Enemy</u>, Ventura, CA., Regal Books, 1992

Dr. Boehm is Available to Speak
To your Church or Organization

Revivals & Evangelistic Meetings

Having preaching revivals and evangelistic meetings in the United States and Haiti, Dr. Boehm is well qualified. If you would like more information and a tape please contact Dr. Boehm.

Children in Danger

A Biblically based presentation designed for adult and youth functions

Adults: The topics arte designed to educate and heighten awareness of dangerous activities our children and teens are constantly being tempted by the world around them to be involved in, why these activities are dangerous, and what can be done. Typically plan on 1 ½ hours not including a time for questions at the conclusion.

Youth: For youth two sessions are recommended which would include a general presentation of approximately 1 to 1 ½ hours. Then the participants would be asked to fill out an anonymous *Spiritual Experience Inventory* which would be compiled. A second session would then be scheduled to discuss specifics related to the experiences of the particular youth group. These sessions could be conducted on the same day.

Our children are playing with fire. On the average, when Christian High School students are surveyed we find these startling results:

45% say they have experienced a "presence" in their room that scared them.

60% say they have harbored bad thoughts about God.

40% find it mentally hard to pray and read their Bible.

70% report hearing "voices" in their head, like there was a subconscious voice talking to them.

20% say they frequently entertain thoughts of suicide.

Both adult and youth presentations would be designed into the time frame of the church or group making the request.

Spiritual Warfare Seminar

A Biblically based presentation designed for church laity

Session topics include: Basic Understanding of Spiritual Warfare; Can a Born Again Believer be demonized?; Spiritual Warfare and the Family; Children in Danger; Problems in Homes, Churches, and other Buildings; Our Victory in Jesus Christ.

Dr. Boehm will tailor presentations to fit your church or group's time schedule and requests. Suggested scheduling might include four evenings 7pm-9pm, or weekend seminar.

All presentation titles can also be presented individually. Dr. Boehm speaks primarily on a love offering basis plus travel and accommodation expenses when out of the area.

For more information or a tailor made presentation or seminar for your church contact:

Dr. Roger Boehm

Center for Christian Counseling & Training

350 N. Washington Avenue, Suite L

Titusville, FL 32796

(321) 269-0404   FAX: (321) 269-8173

E-mail: cfcc@lwol.com

Website: cfcct.org